Lake Arrowhead

CHRONICLES

Lake Arrowhead
CHRONICLES

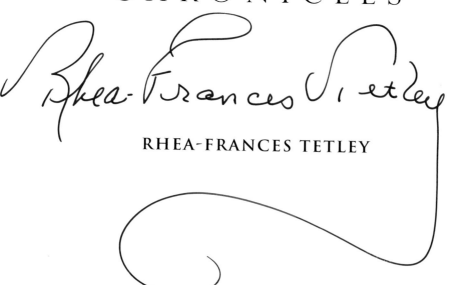

RHEA-FRANCES TETLEY

THE
History
PRESS

Published by The History Press
Charleston, SC 29403
www.historypress.net

Front cover, top: Lake Arrowhead beauties in the 1920s. *Photo by Tony Burke, courtesy of Dr. Don Adkins. Bottom*: Lake Arrowhead in 2014. *Mountain Magick Photography by Kelly Pajak.*

Back cover, top: Lake Arrowhead Club sailboats in the 1980s. *Author's collection. Bottom*: Lake Arrowhead Village in the 1940s. *Author's collection.*

First published 2014

Manufactured in the United States

ISBN 978.1.62619.516.5

Library of Congress Control Number: 2014953183

Contents

Foreword

Though born and raised in Whittier, California, Rhea-Frances Tetley, granddaughter and great-granddaughter of pioneer mountain-area subdividers and developers Frank A. Tetley Sr. and Frank A. Tetley Jr., spent many weekends and summers visiting her family's log cabin vacation home in Crestline. During these childhood visits, she explored the surrounding forest and lakes, falling in love with the mountains and vowing to reside there someday. Rhea-Frances's childhood dream came true in July 1976, when we, recently married college sweethearts, decided to settle down in the family mountain cabin and raise a family of our own.

As a child, Rhea-Frances learned, firsthand, from her father, grandfather and great-aunt about the various mountain communities. This only whetted her appetite for history and led her to acquire a BA in history and a subsequent MA in education to share her passion for history with others. Rhea-Frances's thirst for historical facts led to the creation of the Crest Forest Historical Society in 1986. In 1994, the Crest Forest group expanded its area of historical interest, becoming the Rim of the World Historical Society.

In addition to writing historical and general news articles for the *Crestline Chronicle* and *The Alpenhorn News* since 2001, as well as authoring three books on local history, over the years, Rhea-Frances has served as president and board member of both the Crest Forest and Rim of the World historical societies and as a docent for the Mountain History

Lake Arrowhead Village today. *Author's collection.*

Museum in Lake Arrowhead. Oh, and in her spare time, Rhea-Frances teaches learning-handicapped middle school students in Redlands. And the rest, as they say, is history.

DOUGLAS W. MOTLEY
Senior Writer
The Alpenhorn News

Acknowledgements

I want to thank so many people for their assistance in the creation of this book. Without the support of the Crest Forest/Rim of the World Historical Society since its beginnings in 1986, these stories would not have been collected. Special thanks go to Tom Powell Jr., W. Lee Cozad, Mary Barlow, Dr. Don Adkins and numerous others for extra help, plus the sharing of their resources and pictures through the years. Without the expertise of historians Pauliena LaFuze, Stan Bellamy, J. Putnam Henck, Ralph Wagner, Russ Keller and numerous others, I would not have such detailed stories. I am grateful for their generous sharing.

Without the support and encouragement of my family—parents Ruth and Dick Tetley, proofreader/editor husband Douglas W. Motley and children David Motley and illustrator Sean Motley—I wouldn't have had time to complete this. Thank you to publisher Dennis Labadie and Rose Wiegand of *The Alpenhorn News* for supporting my weekly history column, "Those Were the Days," from which this book is derived.

Thank you friends and co-workers, especially Kay Roberts, for tolerating my connections of all situations to our local history. You are very special.

Introduction

This book is composed of columns written about the history of Lake Arrowhead and the surrounding San Bernardino Mountains. These columns, under the umbrella title "Those Were the Days," appeared in *The Alpenhorn News*.

Collectively, they tell the story of the development of Lake Arrowhead as a community and a resort and detail many issues that local residents faced and overcame.

1
The Native American Era

THE ARROWHEAD

How did the name "Arrowhead" become connected with the San Bernardino mountaintop area? The lake isn't shaped like an arrowhead, so why was the Arrowhead name chosen?

Lake Arrowhead is named after a large scar on the southern slope of the San Bernardino Mountains next to Waterman Canyon and above a series of hot springs adjacent to the San Andreas Fault. This small area of land has been carefully documented and frequently written about, although nothing important ever actually happened on that steep hillside. But its unusual shape and location above hot springs have attracted attention since early Native American days.

The Arrowhead is visible for thirty miles across the valley. It looks somewhat triangular, with the point down toward the natural hot springs below it. It is a quarter of a mile long (1,375 feet) and a furlong wide (449 feet), covering seven and a half acres.

The mark is an outcropping of white quartz with light gray granite soil, so only white sage and other light gray-green vegetation grows on it. This contrasts with the darker earth and thick black-green chaparral that naturally surrounds it.

The Arrowhead's origins are unclear. The scar may have been formed by a gigantic, localized cloudburst that fell, causing a slippage of topsoil.

The Arrowhead Landmark on the mountain's southern face originated these Native American legends and inspired the name of Lake Arrowhead. *Illustration by Sean Motley.*

Or perhaps the contrasted area was the bottom of a waterfall, as other geologists have theorized.

When creating an upscale image for the area, the Arrowhead Lake Company chose a name that would have immediate name recognition: "Lake Arrowhead."

NATIVE AMERICAN LEGENDS OF THE ARROWHEAD

Native Americans have always known the Great Spirit created the seven-and-a-half-acre Arrowhead scar on the mountainside. Each tribe had its own story explaining the reason for its creation and the lesson it taught. Here are two of the stories.

Guachina Tribe Legend

Many years ago, the San Bernardino Valley Indians called the area *Guachina*, meaning "Place of Plenty," referring to the fertility of the soil and the abundance of water. They called themselves Guachina and became arrogant toward others because of this abundance.

The Great Spirit became displeased with their arrogance, sending a fierce Heat Spirit, which caused a drought and blighted their fields. The earth became parched, and all green vegetation shriveled; still, the blasting heat continued. Their herds died from the lack of food and water. They prayed for relief, making peace offerings to the gods, but the heat and famine continued. Finally, bowing in prayer, they offered any sacrifice for the end of their suffering and promised to be forever humble.

Ne-wah-na, the chief's maiden daughter, was beloved by the tribe. A voice floated from the heavens: "Give Ne-wah-na as an offering to heaven." The distraught chief sadly wrapped his only daughter in her richest robes, adorned her with gold trinkets and allowed her to be sacrificed to the Heat Spirit.

Afterward, the heavens opened up, and a white arrow of light struck down the Heat Spirit. Another arrow struck the side of the mountain, leaving its mark to remind them of the famine days and their prior arrogance toward the Great Spirit and their neighbors.

Then the rain fell, filling the streams with water. The Heat Spirit writhed in agony as the earth opened and swallowed him. As it closed, hot, boiling water bubbled up from the spot. The Guachina began to drink and bathe in the steaming waters and were healed from the illnesses brought by the drought.

The tribe kept its promise, remained humble and became the most generous among its neighbors, living for generations in peace and prosperity in the bountiful valley, with the Arrowhead on the hillside reminding them of both their ordeal and promises.

Cahuilla Tribal Legend

The peaceful Cahuilla tribe lived beyond the mountains to the east. Their not-so-peaceful Indian neighbors stole their ponies and food, the latter often while it was still growing in the fields, and harassed them. The Cahuilla were unhappy and called on the "god of peace" to help them find a better place to dwell. The Great Spirit looked favorably on these peaceful people and told them to go west and watch for a sign.

One moonless night, there appeared a "flaming arrow of light" that seemed to embed itself in the mountainside. When the morning light appeared, the tribe saw the Arrowhead emblazoned on the mountainside. There, they lived peacefully in the foothills in the shadow of the Arrowhead until the coming of the white settlers.

DISCOVERY OF THE ARROWHEAD

Spanish explorers mentioned the scar in Father Dumez's journals in 1810, but they saw it as more significant when they named the area San Bernardino. Their journals documented that the Native Americans used the hot and cold springs below the Arrowhead as a sacred healing place.

The first American visitors who saw the scar thought it looked like an upside-down ace of spades. The early Mormon settlers claimed the Arrowhead was the symbol from Brigham Young's visions, pointing to the location for their new settlement.

When San Bernardino County was formed in 1853, the Arrowhead was chosen as its identifying symbol, and it was used on the county seal and logos.

The Arrowhead has burned many times during recorded history. It was burned in 1885 and again in 1895, when two different Arrowhead Springs Hotels were destroyed by fire. Wildfires also ravaged the area in 1916, 1922, 1938, 1943, 1953, 1958, 1970, 1975, the 1980 Panorama Fire, the Arrowhead Fire in 2002 and the Old Fire in October 2003.

Fires destroy the root system of the plants, and erosion occurs if heavy rains fall before the plants can re-grow. An erosion scar began developing on the west side of the Arrowhead after the 1922 fire. In the mid-1920s, the San Bernardino Kiwanis Club used shovels to create a natural brush system of check dams to stop further erosion. Unfortunately, the erosion continued.

The 1950s were a time of life or death for the Arrowhead. Max Green of Mountain Auto Stage Line led the 1950s Arrowhead Preservation Committee, organized to save the Arrowhead from total erosion. To preserve it, more than one hundred small check dams made of steel beams and panels were installed.

In the mid-1950s, the U.S. Forest Service also planted one thousand seedling sumacs around the perimeter of the Arrowhead to improve its visibility to the public. The sumac defined the outline of the Arrowhead and slowed the erosion by growing into a five-foot-tall hedge, but the fires in 1958, '70, '75, '80 and 2002 have proven the sumac isn't fire resistant.

Fears that a mineral claim might be filed on the landmark and excavated forced the Forest Service to declare, in January 1957, that the Arrowhead was a Geologic Landmark Area, preventing its commercial exploitation.

In 1972, the Arrowhead was declared a California Point of Historical Interest. In 1981, San Bernardino National Forest supervisor Bob Tyrrel announced plans to put decorative lighting around the Arrowhead so it could be seen at night, but that never occurred. In January 1988, a grass-roots community group, the Friends of the Arrowhead, spearheaded by Willard Monninger, entered into a partnership with the Forest Service "to preserve, maintain and enhance the Arrowhead Landmark."

The Official Arrowhead Viewing Site, with a granite and marble monument marker and an informational brass plaque at Forty-fourth Street and Waterman Avenue, was established. The two hundred or so check dams are visible with binoculars from the Official Viewing Site. Geologists now believe that the check dams don't actually prevent any erosion. However, their removal would absolutely cause severe erosion to occur. The brass plaque was stolen in 2010, the bicentennial year of the naming of San Bernardino, and replaced with a smaller marble marker by Mr. Monninger just months before his death.

NATIVE AMERICANS IN LITTLE BEAR VALLEY

Just as the mountains are a lure today to those seeking to escape the blistering heat of summer, they also beckoned the Paiute, Mojave and Serrano Indians as a refuge from summer in the desert.

Serrano is the Spanish word for "mountain people." They called themselves *Yuhaviat*, or "the people of the pines." They journeyed up the north side of the mountains each spring. Numerous family groups lived peacefully together, staying until early fall after the gathered acorns were processed. They left the granaries full, allowing the snow to leach out the bitter oils, and stashed their grinding stones and essentials between the rocks.

Archaeologists have excavated several Serrano sites. The most extensively studied location is Indian Rock Camp near Willow Creek, north of Lake Arrowhead. The Lake Arrowhead Women's Club recognized it as a historic site in the 1930s. In the 1960s, the county museum documented that the site had been used for over five thousand summers.

The Serranos lived a nomadic lifestyle, following the ripening seeds and nuts. What may have attracted them to Rock Camp were the natural

The metates at Rock Camp and in the meadow beyond are significantly important to the area's pre-history. *Author's collection.*

depressions in the boulders, which, over generations of use, became metate holes in the granite. These rock outcroppings were next to a perfect camping meadow and stream.

The metates were used with manos (hand stones) for grinding acorns into flour for *wi-wish*, a traditional mush-type food. The Serranos lived among the Coulter and Jeffrey pines, manzanita bushes and black oaks, harvesting acorns, piñon nuts, sage and wild berries and hunting small game and deer. Except for a few large animals (grizzly and black bears, mountain lions, et cetera), there was little danger for the natives. They lived a tranquil lifestyle in a land of plenty, enjoying their free time playing games and singing.

The mountain's Serrano Indians were not disturbed by the Spanish rancheros in the valley in the early 1800s because the Spanish rarely ventured into the mountains and never stayed long. The desert Indians, mostly the Mojaves and Paiutes, had been a problem for the Mexican ranchero owners for decades, as outlaw native bands frequently stole horses and cattle from the rancheros.

The Mojaves and Paiutes got angrier when the "invasion" of white lumbermen moved into the mountains. They believed their traditional hunting grounds were being stolen from them. During the 1860s, the desert tribes vowed to drive out these white interlopers who were building permanent structures, bothering the game in their hunting and gathering grounds and cutting the trees.

The Serranos would probably still be living their traditional lives if not for the loggers who arrived in the 1850s. The Battle of Indian Hill took place between Blue Jay and Little Bear Valley when some Paiute Indians came up the mountain on January 29, 1867, to reclaim their ancient hunting grounds. This three-day-long series of skirmishes resulted in the burning of the Benson-Pine Sawmill (Burnt Mill) and the looting and torching of William Kane's cabin. After the two-hour battle, the Paiutes retreated to the desert.

Many whites decided it was time to eliminate the "Indian problem." An armed sheriff's posse spent thirty-two days going through the mountains removing all Native Americans. They mistook the peaceful Serranos for the aggressive Paiutes, thus exiling them from their ancestral lands.

To protect his people, Santos Manuel gathered the remaining Valley and Mountain Serrano Indians and led them to the foothills just a few miles east of the Arrowhead, to a remote mountain foothill area, safely away from the white man. It would be another ten years before President Grant, in 1876, set aside that land for them.

The San Manuel Band of Mission Indians was recognized in 1891 and guaranteed their reservation location in the southern foothills of the San Bernardino Mountains. Following generations of living in poverty on the small, sparsely resourced hillside, they now operate a casino and donate generously to the community.

2
The Logging Era

The Legacy of Francis (Frank) Talmadge Sr. and Family

The story of the life of Francis (Frank) Talmadge is full of adventure, hard work, financial success and a legacy of presence in the mountain area into the middle of the twentieth century.

Francis Talmadge decided to take a short working vacation in 1853 after leading a wagon train trek from St. Louis to San Bernardino, and that short two weeks changed mountain history.

Talmadge arrived in San Bernardino after spending eight months on the trail, supplying the wagon train with fresh meat, which he shot with his two-barrel, muzzleloading rifle, named Foxsong.

A mountain man, Talmadge saw the wooded San Bernardino Mountains and felt he needed the coolness of the trees after his long desert trip. He spent two weeks working at the Seely Sawmill in the current-day Valley of Enchantment before moving to El Monte. There, the skilled hunter and adventurous young man began farming and transporting freight.

While in El Monte, Talmadge married Firnetta Jane Strong (Nettie), a widowed woman with three children. They met on a wagon train he had led west to Sacramento a few years earlier.

In 1862, after the birth of his first son, Will, Frank moved his whole family up to the San Bernardino Mountains, where he became a key player in the Little Bear Valley lumber industry over the next twenty-five years.

He arrived just after the horrible Noachian Flood winter storm of 1862 that had washed out parts of the old Mormon Road and destroyed several sawmills, including the David Seely Mill, where Talmadge had worked nine years before.

Frank began hauling lumber down the mountain for the James Rowland Steam Sawmill located on James Flat, currently under Lake Gregory. He helped Jerome Benson and Sam Pine construct the first sawmill (Benson-Pine Mill) in Little Bear Valley. His second son, John, was born in the family cabin in 1864, becoming the first white child to be born in Little Bear Valley. Mountain life agreed with John; he grew up and worked as a cowboy in the mountains until his death at age ninety-one.

Frank Talmadge also helped build the large (James) Caley Mill near present-day Blue Jay in 1865. Two years later, he filed his own timber claims on 320 acres of forestland on the west side of Little Bear Valley, building his first sawmill.

It was while doing repairs in January 1867 at the seasonally closed Caley Mill that things were noticed to be "missing." The losses were thefts by a renegade war party of Paiute Indians that had entered the area through Little Bear Gorge from the desert side of the mountain. Unknown to the loggers, the Little Bear Valley area was the Indians' ancient hunting and gathering grounds. The Indians did not want to share and did not intend on allowing the increasing number of lumbermen and their families to remain on their land.

One January day, while Bill Caine was at the Caley Mill making repairs, a Paiute Indian war party came into the valley and discovered Caine's cabin, which upset them because it was physical proof of the intruders' intent to remain in the area. The natives looted all the valuables, including food, provisions, blankets and Caine's rifle, and then burned the cabin to the ground. Next, they took Caine's cattle and drove them down the gorge through the snowdrifts.

As they drove the cattle past the seasonally closed Benson-Pine Mill, the Paiutes also looted and burned that mill to the ground. The name Burnt Mill in the area comes from this 1867 episode.

The burning of the Benson-Pine Mill and Bill Caine's cabin (not far from Talmadge's own family cabin) angered Talmadge and the Little Bear Valley lumbermen who had invested their money and lived in the sawmills. This resulted in a quickly organized group of men led by Talmadge, along with Caine, Jonathan Richards and George Armstrong, chasing the Paiutes on horseback. They caught up to eight of them between where the Willow

The Benson-Talmadge Sawmill. *Author's collection.*

Creek tunnel and Hamiltaire are today. Shots were fired, and Cain's horse was shot out from under him, causing him to lose his only other rifle in the snow. Talmadge hid behind a large tree, shooting and killing an Indian. This, of course, angered the Paiutes even more.

Another Indian, knowing Talmadge would not have enough time to reload a gun, leapt out at Talmadge, preparing to fire on him. But Foxsong was a two-barrel shotgun, so Frank fired again and killed the surprised Indian instantly. The war party soon retreated, and the lumbermen returned to Talmadge's Mill and fortified it while Richards used the back roads to quickly get down to San Bernardino to summon help.

The next morning, a small scouting party of lumbermen discovered Caine's dropped rifle and the location of the Paiutes. With reinforcements, Talmadge's "army" of about ten to twelve lumbermen found fifty to sixty Paiutes climbing up a ridge above Little Bear Creek, intending to ambush the lumbermen and drive them out of their hunting grounds once and for all.

Over one hundred shots were fired during the two-hour Battle of Indian Hill. During the battle, two lumbermen were wounded; Bill Caine received a ball in his leg, and John Welty was hit with an arrow to the shoulder. One Indian was killed and at least another six injured before they retreated to the desert. The lumbermen returned to Talmadge's sawmill and tended to their wounded. This was the last time the Indians

The Talmadge Sawmill in 1892. *Author's collection.*

attacked any property in the mountain area. A sheriff's posse then cleared the mountains of all Indians.

Talmadge filed timber claims on another 320 acres of state school land located in Little Bear Meadow that cost him $1.25 an acre, for a total of $400.00. By 1876, he had 980 acres of land that he was haying (to feed the work animals), lumbering and living on. That October, Talmadge held a gala housewarming and mill-raising party; folks came to help raise his new mill frame.

The next year, 1877, Talmadge invited everyone from the mountain to attend a party to celebrate the new house built for his wife, Nettie, and their six children. The Talmadge parties were always festive affairs, as the family often built a dance floor for the festivities.

The highlight of 1879 was the wedding of Talmadge's daughter, Edna, to Charles Daley, son of Edward Daley, patriarch of the road-building family from Del Rosa. Edward Daley, in 1870, had built the Daley Canyon Road, which linked Little Bear Valley sawmills directly to the valley below.

Agreements were made among the lumbermen in the 1880s to set prices that would be fair to all so everyone could make money. In 1881, the price for common lumber was to be twenty-seven dollars per thousand linear feet, and the price for clear lumber was set at thirty-five dollars. That year was very successful, as the mountaintop sawmills milled about four million feet of lumber, with most of it pre-sold or cut under a contract before it ever reached San Bernardino.

The sawmills of William LaPraix, Ernst Somers, Hudson & Taylor, the Tyler brothers and the Talmadge family produced over six million feet of lumber in 1883.

The Talmadge Sawmill was a real family operation. By 1886, Talmadge had all three of his sons managing various operations at the mill. Eldest son Will (aka Teet) was in charge of loading the logs onto the solid-wheeled logging wagon and transporting them to the mill. After the wood was milled, middle son John (aka Peg) oversaw moving the lumber down the narrow Daley Canyon Road to San Bernardino, managing the drivers. Frank Jr., Talmadge's youngest son (aka Fish), was in charge of the day-to-day operations of the mill.

The problem of getting the lumber to market was becoming even more difficult because of the declining quality of the roads. The 1870 Daley Road was getting old, was steep and had many sharp curves, which were difficult to manage with a full wagonload of lumber, and despite yearly grading and repairs, it was rutted and wearing out.

In 1887, a narrow-gauge railroad route to haul lumber to the bottom of the mountain was proposed. Sawmill owners Talmadge, along with LaPraix, the Tyler brothers and John Waters, formed a company to build that rail line to San Bernardino from Little Bear Valley. The first two miles of the narrow-gauge line were constructed in San Bernardino, paralleling Baseline Avenue. Known as the San Bernardino, Arrowhead and Waterman Railroad, it was designed to go up Smith (Waterman) Canyon to the crest and then turn east to Little Bear Meadow, where the Talmadge Mill was

Frank Talmadge's meadow, where he raised hay for his work animals, is now under Lake Arrowhead. *Author's collection.*

located. It was predicted that the rail line would open up the forests and lower the cost of getting the lumber to the valley.

The rail project was not successful; none of the rail bed up the mountain was ever constructed. The problem was that the route was designed using Smith Canyon. Although it was the first road up the mountain in the 1850s, the Mormon Road to the crest had gone through that canyon but had been washed out by the 1867 Noachian Deluge and abandoned. Robert W. Waterman had purchased the land. As California's governor, Waterman refused to allow any roads to be built through his canyon and risk polluting his pure water. The dream of a logging train route to Little Bear Valley died.

A few years later, in 1891, after the death of retired governor Waterman, the Arrowhead Reservoir Company (ARC) announced it had purchased all the land in Little Bear and Grass Valleys and intended to create a water project on the land. The financially flush company also purchased a right of way through Waterman Canyon from the governor's heirs and built an expensive wagon toll road through the canyon to the crest of the mountain.

Talmadge's Little Bear properties were included in the ARC land deal. Because of his deal, he was allowed to continue operating his mill in the same area where he had been sawing for twenty years, removing trees from the area for the ARC until the mill was destroyed by fire in 1894. He suffered a $20,000 loss to his buildings and equipment, but had only a $2,000 insurance policy. This was the end of Frank Talmadge Sr.'s logging business.

Talmadge retired to Victorville. His unique reputation as a pioneer lumberman, Indian fighter and wagon train scout preceded him. He and Nettie were welcomed and became well-respected members of the community until her death in 1910 and his, at the age of eighty-eight, in 1918.

Talmadge's sons stayed on the mountain, running herds of cattle in Big Bear until the area became too populated for grazing. Everyone in the family was respected. When Will's two sons drowned in Big Bear Lake in 1909, more than six hundred people attended the funeral in San Bernardino. It was 1923 when the brothers sold part of their 750,000-acre IS Ranch to developer Albert Spalding, who developed the area known as Moonridge in current-day Big Bear.

The family continued to ranch in the area by leasing grazing land. Through the mid-1950s, the IS Ranch cattle drives collected the grazing cattle from across the San Bernardino Mountains. The roundups continued the family tradition of big parties and fun, including daytime cattle branding and nighttime dancing.

The entire Talmadge family on a picnic in the 1890s in Little Bear Valley. *Author's collection.*

The Talmadge sons lived long lives in the San Bernardino Mountains. Eldest son Will lived to be eighty-three, dying in 1945. Middle son John (the first white baby born in Little Bear Valley, now Lake Arrowhead) lived to be ninety-one, dying in 1955, and the youngest son, Frank Jr., died at age eighty-three.

The San Bernardino Mountains were changed significantly by the almost one hundred years that the colorful Talmadge family lived there.

EDWARD DALEY'S ROAD OPENED LITTLE BEAR VALLEY

Transportation is the key factor in being able to live or work on the mountain. On Highway 18, there is a wooden oxen yoke sitting on a rock base, just east of Rimforest. California Historical Monument #570 denotes where the Daley Toll Road, which ran from Del Rosa to the crest near Strawberry Peak and then down to the mills in Agua Fria, Blue Jay and Little Bear Valley, crossed the current highway.

This oxen yoke monument is state Historical Marker #570 and sits at the intersection of current State Highway 18 and the Old Daley Wagon Toll Road. *Photo by Rhea-Frances Tetley.*

It is a monument to the dirt roads of the 1870s, constructed by the Daley family, and recognizes the dangerous route teamsters used to transport the lumber off the mountain.

During the sawmill days, from 1853 to 1905, lumbermen used fourteen different roads into the mountains to access the timber. These roads had steep grades and were built and owned by the lumber companies that created them. Those early lumber wagons' brakes were severely stressed by the up to 25 percent grades of those early roads, such as the Mormon Lumber Road, built up Smith Canyon in 1853 (named for Joseph Smith the founder of the Mormon faith). The steepness of the roads is the reason some lumber wagons dragged the tops of trees behind them to prevent runaways of the heavily loaded wagons as they went downhill.

One early San Bernardino road builder Edward Barber Daley Sr. was also one of San Bernardino's city founders and a county supervisor in the 1880s. He married Nancy Ann Hunt, daughter of Captain Jefferson Hunt, before they came to San Bernardino in 1851. Captain Hunt, along with Amasa Lyman and David Seely, led the three sections of the wagon train of Mormons to California to start the Mormon colony at San Bernardino.

Much of the San Bernardino colony's early road construction was entrusted to the supervision of Edward Daley. He and his father-in-law and sons directed the building of the 1853 Mormon Lumber Road up Smith (aka Waterman) Canyon to access the trees in the Seely and Huston Flats areas (future Crestline) and to acquire logs for the stockade to protect the colony from Native Americans in San Bernardino.

After the Mormon Road washed out twice, Edward Daley and his sons built a better road to access the mid-range valleys where the lumbermen had moved their mills. In 1870, the Daley Road Company was incorporated for a period of twenty years, with the stock selling for $240 a share. It was a safer and less dangerous road than the previous ones available. The twelve-foot-wide, steep road had only 10 to 15 percent grades, which were considered not difficult for horse- or oxen-pulled wagons. This improved road was named the Mountain Turnpike, or the Twin and City Creek Toll Road. It ended in Del Rosa at the Daley family ranch, making collecting tolls easier.

This was the road used for transporting lumber from the Little Bear area through current-day Blue Jay, giving lumbermen a better road that opened the mid-range of the mountains to commercial lumbering. This was the road the Caley, Tyler, Talmadge, LaPraix and other Little Bear Valley mills used. It took a good teamster about six to seven hours to complete the one-way trip on the road.

The first lumber moved down the new road in April/May 1870, after the snows melted and the mills began to reopen.

A grand-opening barbecue party was held on July 4 of that year, with many speeches by local politicians, including former and future county supervisors and assemblymen and respected lumbermen, and a brass band, and it concluded with an uninvited thunderstorm.

"The Turnpike" was hailed as "a convenience never before known, and would make the mountains a favorite place of resort, being accessible by almost any kind of vehicle," stated the *Guardian* newspaper in San Bernardino.

The next day, signs displaying the toll rates went up at the upper and lower tollhouses. The one-way rate for wagons and two horses was thirty-seven and a half cents, while wagons with six horses were charged sixty-two cents (they could eat more grass along the way). Carriages (usually filled with the tourists that lumbermen wanted to avoid) were fifty cents, sheep (they usually were brought in herds anyway) were five cents, cattle or horses were fifty cents and single horsemen and pack animals were charged twenty-five cents. The road was the most direct route to transport lumber to the valley below from the sawmills located in and around Little Bear Valley.

The upper tollhouse, run by John Commerford, was located in the trees just north of the crest. Known as Old John's Saloon, it sold tobacco, liquor and playing cards. The restaurant's actual name was Old John Commerford's Tollhouse Tavern. It provided food, refreshments and a place to relax after the long drive or while preparing for it. Old John's was known for the wrestling matches held there among teamsters as a diversion between loads and as a place for a last drink before the perilous trip back down into the San Bernardino Valley. The stop before going down the mountain was usually shorter—generally meaning without too much alcohol—as the driver had to be in total control of his horse team while negotiating that road or the entire load could be lost.

The Daley Toll Road was the widest and safest way up to that time to access the mountain. The road, although better than previous ones, still had sharp curves and steep cliffs. Keeping the team under control while going down the steep downhill sections or meeting face-to-face with an uphill wagon on the twelve-foot-wide road was dangerous for all. About thirty wagons a day used the Daley Road. Despite the steep cliff along its edge and the sharp curves, it was over a year before any accident was recorded there.

By the mid-1870s, loggers' family members were coming up the mountain during the summers to camp and enjoy the cooler mountain air, thus escaping the sizzling heat in the valley. These families and their friends could be considered the first summertime vacationing families to enjoy the Little Bear area.

By the mid-1890s, most of the mills either had been bought by the Arrowhead Reservoir Company or closed, owing to the construction of Little Bear Lake and the creation of the National Forest Preserve in 1891. The Arrowhead Reservoir Toll Road (two dollars), a newer, wider, lesser-grade road with fewer sharp curves, opened through Waterman Canyon in 1892, so the Daley Road lost some of its public appeal, although its tolls remained much lower.

Road builder Edward B. Daley Sr. had eleven children, eight of whom lived to adulthood. When the Mormons were recalled to Salt Lake City in 1858, Daley stayed in San Bernardino, becoming a successful farmer.

Daley was later elected Third District county supervisor, serving from 1880 to 1883. The family had a large farm in Del Rosa, and Edward Daley Jr. sold part of it to the state for the construction of a new state hospital during their friend Robert Waterman's term as California governor. The hospital eventually developed into Patton State Hospital. Edward Daley was well liked in the community and respected for his concern for others' welfare. He died in 1896 at the age of seventy-one.

The Daley Road Monument was placed on the Rim of the World High Gear Road on July 4, 1935, just after it was completed, by the Arrowhead #110 and Lugonia #271 parlors of the Native Sons and Daughters of the Golden West. The plaque states:

The Daley Road (aka Twin and City Creek Toll Road), built up from Del Rosa, opened the Little Bear Valley (Lake Arrowhead) area to lumbering in the 1870s. The monument marks the location where the road crossed the crest.

The monument was recognized as a state historical landmark in 1957. Without Daley's Toll Road, the Little Bear Valley area would have been much more difficult to log in the 1870s.

JAMES/CALEY SAWMILL: BLUE JAY

Sawmills began to move into Little Bear Valley in the early 1860s. The first reference to the current Blue Jay area was in the spring of 1862 when a grizzly bear (Old Dinah) and her mean cub (Mormon Elder) were captured at Little Bear Creek. The log trap box was baited with a cattle head by lumberman Frank Talmadge and Doc Foster, who transported the bears to El Monte for bear-versus-bull fights. Old Dinah defeated twelve Spanish bulls, with her thirteenth ending in a double death.

When Jonathan James relocated his steam sawmill from Huston Flat down to what was to later become the Crestline area in 1865, he chose to reconstruct the mill next to Little Bear Creek to supply the water for his steam engine. He hired William Caley to help operate one of the first circular steam-powered saw blades on the mountain.

After James was elected to the state legislature in 1866, Caley, along with partners Jonathan Richardson and Isaac Roper, purchased the James sawmill for $5,000 in gold coins and one-third of the lumber cut for three years. It was during the winter of 1867, while the Caley Mill was closed, that Frank Talmadge noticed that the Paiutes had stolen items from the mill, leading to the Battle of Indian Hill. James served in the legislature until 1869, and then he returned and reentered the sawmill business nearby in Grass Valley.

Daley Canyon Road was the major lumbering and supply road into the mountains beginning in 1870. The dusty wagon road paralleled Little Bear Creek down from the crest and Old John's Saloon and went past the Caley Mill.

Caley and his partners operated their sawmill until Caley's untimely death, after being kicked by a mule in 1877. The mill continued to operate into the 1880s. The Little Bear Creek area developed into the Camp Blue Jay fishing camp (1907) and was later purchased by the Wixoms in 1914.

TYLER BROTHERS SAWMILL: GRASS VALLEY

Grass Valley now refers to the area surrounding the Lake Arrowhead Country Club Golf Course. In 1870, former assemblyman Jonathan James entered into a partnership with Dudley Dickey and opened the first lumber mill in that area. The James/Dickey Sawmill was sold several times. On October 7, the mill caught fire, destroying the mill, equipment and five thousand feet of cut lumber.

Joseph Tyler, who had been lumbering in the mountain area for years, urged his brother Charles to move his family to the San Bernardino Mountains, and together they would buy and rebuild the burned-out James and Dickey Sawmill. Charles named the area "Grass Valley" after leaving the Northern California gold fields of the same name. He paid $1,000 in gold coins in December 1870. John James helped them rebuild a larger mill, with a muley saw for splitting logs and a circular saw for lumber. The mill once cut a log seventy-four inches in diameter. The seventh green of the Lake Arrowhead Country Club Golf Course is the approximate location of the Tyler brothers' steam-powered sawmill.

Lumber being taken to market along the Daley Road from the Tyler Brothers Grass Valley Sawmill. *Photo by H.B. Wesner; courtesy Stan Bellamy.*

Charles and Joseph Tyler were the first white men "on record" to use skis in the San Bernardino Mountains. In his diaries, Joseph Tyler wrote of using skis during the winter to get provisions. Charles, who had been mining gold in the northern Grass Valley of the Sierra Nevadas, taught Joseph how to cross-country ski. Those skis he used were probably ten feet long and more than four inches wide. It can be assumed that during the 1870s and '80s, a few other loggers and miners who remained in the mountains during the winter also used skis and sleds, as they were practical during the snowy months. The Tylers operated the mill until 1891, when the mill and land were sold to the Arrowhead Reservoir Company.

The Grass Valley Tunnel was completed in 1907 for the Arrowhead Reservoir and Power Company. That tunnel was dug to allow water to flow from Little Bear Lake and be stored in a reservoir on its way to San Bernardino. The planned reservoir would have filled the entire valley where the Lake Arrowhead Country Club Golf Course is now located.

The San Bernardino National Forest (SBNF) was established in 1925. The Clark-McNary Acts of 1924 and 1925 provided funds to protect the national forests by doing preventative actions, such as building firebreaks and lookout towers. The first SBNF fire lookout tower built was on the ridge west of Grass Valley in June 1925 and was manned during the fire seasons.

The tall, wooden Grass Valley Lookout Tower collapsed during strong winds and heavy snows in the winter of 1933. The metal Strawberry Peak Lookout was built to replace it.

The Grass Valley Tunnel is still used to fill Grass Valley Lake, which has a lakeside playground near the golf course, one of the numerous amenities available to Arrowhead Woods property owners.

LAPRAIX SAWMILLS

The former head sawyer for the Knight and Dickey Sawmill in 1860, William Stewart LaPraix bought that sawmill's equipment, moved it and opened the Excelsior Sawmill in Little Bear Valley on property he had bought from Francis Avery. LaPraix was also a blacksmith, a service that was in high demand among the mill operators, as their equipment broke frequently. It is said he had the best blacksmith shop on the mountaintop. He also spent the winters cutting and storing ice, which would be shipped to the valley floor. When citrus fruit began to be shipped eastward by train, the ice was in

The grave of William LaPraix in Pioneer Cemetery in San Bernardino. *Photo by Rhea-Frances Tetley.*

even higher demand. LaPraix's Excelsior Sawmill was not his only mill, as he also bought equipment and built one in Cedar Flats in partnership with the Tyler brothers in 1879.

In 1881, the lumber mill owners banded together, printing price schedules for lumber brought out of the San Bernardino Mountains so all would make a profit and were not undercutting one another's prices. That year, four million linear feet of lumber were removed from the mountains and sold as fast as they were cut.

LaPraix sold his Little Bear Valley mill equipment in 1881 to Van Slyke, and then he bought out the Tyler brothers' partnership, disassembled that Seely Flat mill and moved it to Little Bear Valley, as the equipment was newer and better. LaPraix and the Tyler brothers were in other partnerships, including ownership of the Snowline Lumberyard in San Bernardino, which they had purchased from Frank Talmadge for $4,000.

LaPraix owned 960 acres of lumber with a value of $1,800 and equipment valued at $1,400 in 1882. In 1885, he moved his mill to a different location in Little Bear Valley, now known as Orchard Bay, to shorten the distance from the mill to the trees he was cutting. His mills continued to be successful. He had a habit of eating apples, and wherever he had a mill, he would plant those apple cores—a local Johnny Appleseed, so to speak. Many apple trees in areas of his former lumber mills are from LaPraix.

In the summer of 1887, LaPraix was killed when he fell into his machinery while working in his Excelsior Sawmill. LaPraix's nephew James Fleming inherited and took over mill operations until he sold his (renamed) Fleming Creek Sawmill to the Arrowhead Reservoir Company in 1891.

3

The Arrowhead Reservoir Project Begins

COLONEL ADOLPH WOOD ADDRESSES SAN BERNARDINO

In the mid-1880s, the town of San Bernardino was known as an outfitting station for mule trains servicing the silver mines in the desert, for being the town at the railroad crossroads and for its proximity to the lumber produced in the mountains and for a little agriculture.

The communities of Highland and Redlands were blooming as ranchers planted groves of citrus trees, since the new Big Bear Dam gave the area a reliable, year-round supply of water for their thriving agricultural industry.

San Bernardino's city engineer, Adolph H. Koebig, was envious of Redlands because Dr. Benjamin Barton had incorporated with others as the Bear Valley Reservoir and Irrigation Company, building a $75,000 dam in Big Bear Valley in 1884 and securing a dependable supply of water that enabled the citrus groves and agricultural industry to flourish.

San Bernardino had underground water, but not enough to sustain agricultural growth. Koebig wanted his town, San Bernardino, to become an agricultural powerhouse, too, but it didn't have a natural flow of water from the mountains to feed the agricultural industry. However, the soil was fertile and ready to be developed.

Koebig and San Bernardino newspaper editor L.H. Holt, who was one of the best practical irrigation men in the county, made many mule trips into the mountains, which were the lumber source for much of the construction growth Southern California was experiencing.

Koebig and Holt examined the mountains and decided that there were several locations that would be excellent for dam projects to send water down to irrigate the fertile San Bernardino Valley. Finding no local funding sources, Robinson J. Jones suggested that Koebig travel to Cincinnati, Ohio, in the spring of 1890 to meet with and convince prospective investors (including Colonel Adolph Wood, Jones's stepfather) that the San Bernardino Valley both needed and wanted an irrigation project.

After that meeting, Colonel Adolph Wood, Benjamin Erhman and Colonel Latham Anderson came quietly to San Bernardino, under the auspices of visiting Jones that autumn, to examine Koebig's claims. Upon their return to Ohio, the Arrowhead Reservoir Company was formed with the intention of building three dams and reservoirs to send eighty thousand acre-feet of water to San Bernardino yearly for irrigation purposes.

The Arrowhead Reservoir Company (ARC), capitalized at $1 million, was composed of prominent Cincinnati businessmen, but it was incorporated across the river in Kentucky because there were significant tax advantages available there in December 1890.

The president of the ARC was James Gamble (of Proctor and Gamble), Mr. Adolph Wood was vice-president and Benjamin Ehrman was secretary. Directors were James Mooney, Charles Kilgour, Henry Lewis, Colonel Latham Anderson and Ellis Potter.

Koebig made numerous trips into the mountains that spring of 1891, building small dams and then filing for those water rights at the San Bernardino County Recorder's Office, preparing for the next step.

Colonel Wood arrived in San Bernardino in May 1891. Koebig and Jones took Colonel Wood up into the mountains, and two weeks later, several real

Adolph H. Koebig. *Author's collection.*

estate transactions had been completed with mountain sawmill owners and others initiated.

Then, Colonel Adolph Wood, as vice-president representing the Arrowhead Reservoir Company, purchased the water rights that Koebig had registered on May 21, 1891, as well as those from Robinson J. Jones, Wood's stepson. On June 1, the company purchased the sawmill and timberland from James Fleming for $26,000 and additional land parcels from J.B. Tyler and John Hook. On June 2, the ARC bought out W.E. Van Slyke. None of the sawmill owners had full knowledge of the future plans of the Arrowhead Reservoir Company or how the company's massive project would significantly impact the mountain area.

The Arrowhead Reservoir project deal became a top story in Holt's June 5, 1891 edition of the *San Bernardino Times Index* newspaper. The article stated:

> *The system will consist of several reservoirs, one of which will be located in Little Bear Valley (future Lake Arrowhead), one in Green Valley (future Grass Valley) and one in Huston Flat (future Crestline) with probably other reservoirs that may be hereafter determined and located. These reservoirs will be filled by means of a large canal to carry winter water from Deep Creek. The reservoirs are each in a separate watershed, but all connected together so they can all be drained into the San Bernardino Valley through a tunnel at the head of Waterman Canyon, or some other point, further west, that may be fixed hereafter...the capacity of the system will be, when completed, sufficient to irrigate 120,000 acres of land.*

The entire irrigation project was expected to be completed by the summer of 1892.

Wood opened an office in San Bernardino, and the town enthusiastically embraced the irrigation reservoir project concept. The City of San Bernardino organized a magnificent banquet to honor Wood and to welcome the Arrowhead Reservoir Company on June 12, 1891. Invitations were sent to all the prominent people of Southern California.

The whole town seemed involved in the banquet festivities. It was an event organized to rival any held previously in San Bernardino and one they hoped would never be equaled. The women spent the day twining the pillars of the Stewart Hotel with honeysuckle and pomegranate blossoms with banks of roses, lilies and ferns that spelled out "Welcome."

When the evening of June 12 arrived, the parlor of the hotel was filled with the two hundred most prominent men of Southern California, and "the discussions were on the wonderful fate that was to befall upon San Bernardino Valley," according to published reports.

The Redlands Orchestra provided the evening's entertainment, and the delicious dinner was filled with "gastronomical delights and fine wines." Judge George E. Otis led the group through a number of toasts honoring the men of the Arrowhead Reservoir Company and especially their guest of honor, Colonel Adolph Wood. They were anxious to hear what Wood had to say, as they realized history was about to be made.

After much toasting, Adolph Wood stood up and spoke:

> *Gentlemen of the city and valley of San Bernardino. You have foregone the comforts of your homes tonight and the indulgence of that rest which is every toiler's due when day's work is done, and have gathered here to celebrate the recent inauguration of an irrigation enterprise undertaken by a number of Cincinnati gentlemen, who have incorporated for that purpose under the name of Arrowhead Reservoir Company, which has for its object the conservation in a series of dams of the water, which falls upon the north side of the Sierra Madre Mountains* [as the San Bernardino Range was known at the time], *lying east of Cajon Pass, whose foothills are within two or three miles of your city limits and which water is to be brought by flume and a tunnel through the crest of these mountains for use in irrigating the dry lands lying south and west of the point of emergence. The water thus diverted is for the most part wasted by the present heat upon the desert sands.* [Applause]

> *In any case, there will be water enough left on that side to provide through our, or some other system, for any possible extension of the cultivation there. The arrest by us of the tremendous water flow of the chief tributary of the Mojave will, we think, be regarded as a partial relief by those residing there, from such damage as resulted last winter when the fierce current lowered the bed of the river from 12 to 23 feet.* [Applause]

> *No man's rights shall knowingly be invaded.* [Applause] *We invoke the aid of every citizen so long as our conduct of the affairs of the company shall not be adverse to your common welfare.*

> *As to our work and the rapidity of its progress—our unfamiliarity with all the physical obstacles render it impossible for us to say how quickly it shall be accomplished. But, it is our hope and belief, based on the estimate of our engineers and the well known capacity of California contractors, that we shall be able to reverse the direction of the mountain streams with which we have to do and cause them to flow into the valley early in the summer of 1892.* [Applause]

Wood then spoke about the Bear Valley Water Project and listed the numerous benefits Redlands had received from the steady flow of year-round water:

Colonel A. Wood, vice-president of the Arrowhead Reservoir Company. His stepson, Robinson Jones, brought the Arrowhead Reservoir project to Ohio seeking investors. *Rhea-Frances Tetley collection.*

Without their example and without the legislation which they and the public spirited citizens of your commonwealth have procured in the passage of the district irrigation laws, reducing the relation of the reservoir system and the landowners to a practical basis, I very much doubt if the bold and audacious experiment of these gentlemen could have been repeated, our people would not have ventured to make the investment now proposed. [Applause]

Its inception and the arduous labor involved in determining its feasibility has been the work of one of your own citizens, mayhap at great personal sacrifice, Mr. A.H. Koebig, who originally undertook the burden of labor and expense and was faithful to the end.

Wood then highly praised San Bernardino on its city improvements under the guidance of city engineer A.H. Koebig. Then, in the final part of his speech, he challenged those two hundred prominent men in attendance to be forward thinking about the future of San Bernardino:

But, with all these wonderful aspects of San Bernardino you do not have some things which I would like to mention that are possible of attainment. [Applause]

I believe you have within your reach an attraction, which could prove to be unique—peculiar only to your city. It is based upon what I regard as the most superb inland view to be obtained in Southern California.

Suppose you were to choose the line of "C" Street from Highland and were to construct a road to the foothills, swerving around the little mountain for variety, thence by a good mountain road, double track, of good grade, to the top of the mountain—which our company will build if permitted—through Waterman Canyon, or "Arrowhead Canyon," if you will.

Thence let someone build a good road partly along and partly behind the crest of the mountain until the new road up City Creek is encountered—thence back by that and Highland Avenue, also beautiful with orange orchards and ornamental trees to the city.

Mayhap, someone would build a small house of entertainment on the mountaintop where tourists might spend the night, and where one might gaze at leisure at what is destined to be the most lively valley in the world when filled, as well it will be, with orchards and vineyards and peaceful villages.

Now I come to a question of more material interest to the growth of this city. Fuel of all kinds is costly here. Fuel is heat, heat is power. It happens that our company, in the prosecution of its park, will have the means of developing an enormous amount of power...

You will see there may be developed without detriment to our original purpose a great manufacturing power. If we harness this power, can it be used to your advantage? [Applause]

Wood outlined many examples of power uses, such as in stamp mills and the making of ice, which was then a luxury, and many more:

As for the ladies, God bless 'em, who have surrounded us with tonight's beauty. Their hand (since we are denied their presence) is grateful to me. May you have many blessed streams of water dedicated to the production of beautiful flowers and shrubs. [Applause]

On June 13, the day after Wood's speech, the ARC bought out lumberman Peter B. Guernsey and two days later completed the last deal with John Suverkrup. The ARC now held title to 4,360 acres of mountain land. It was prepared to proceed and divert the direction of the mountain streams from the Mojave River watershed to the San Bernardino Valley.

The 1890s started out as an era when anything was considered possible, and with the economic boom the country was experiencing, patriotic men were willing to invest in massive projects. Perhaps if the project had been built according to the original specifications, all would have gone well, but the ARC expanded the plan from the three-dam and three-lake project to include seven dams and lakes with connecting tunnels instead of canals. Its initial $1 million capitalization could not fund such a grand vision.

CONSTRUCTION OF LITTLE BEAR VALLEY DAM: NINETEENTH CENTURY

When the Arrowhead Reservoir Company offered to pay cash for the various sawmills in the Little Bear Valley area, the sawmill owners, without conferring with one another, quickly sold their lands to the new company. After all, the National Forest Reserve was forming, and the mill owners expected they would be forced to close soon, anyway.

The Koebig reservoir proposal was well planned and extensive. It was to be a three-reservoir project (Little Bear, Huston Flat and Green Valley). Each of the lakes was in a different watershed, so more water could be gathered, and would be joined together by gravity-flow canals. The water would be sent to the San Bernardino Valley through a tunnel built near the top of Waterman Canyon. It was estimated that this water could irrigate 120,000 acres of land in the valley areas, possibly as far west as Pasadena.

There was great enthusiasm for the project, as the company predicted the water would be ready to flow to the valley in the summer of 1892. If the project had been built as originally designed, the current lakes—Lake Arrowhead, Lake Gregory and Grass Valley Lake—would be drastically larger in size, deeper and in different locations than they are currently so they would hold more water.

But the plans were almost immediately enlarged to a seven-lake project, designing additional water storage reservoirs in Seeley Flat (now Valley of Enchantment), the Las Flores Ranch in Summit Valley, Deep Creek and Cedar Springs (now Silverwood Lake), then known as the Mojave River Reservoir.

The Little Bear Reservoir project was heralded as one of the largest and most ambitious water projects in California. The streams that were to be dammed—Little Bear Creek, Holcombe Creek, Crab Creek, Deep Creek, Huston Creek and Hook Creek, along with others—were to directly flow into the reservoirs.

The Arrowhead Reservoir Company's plan to send water to San Bernardino was a massive, many-faceted project. It required roads and

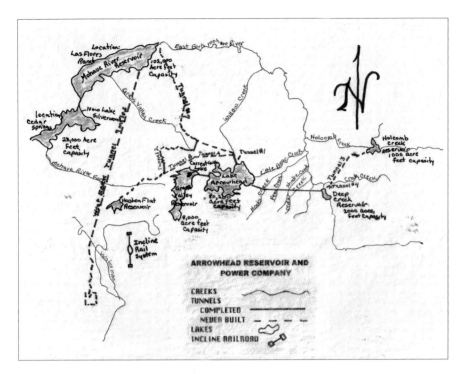

Hand-drawn map of the proposed Seven-Lake Project of the Arrowhead Reservoir Company. *Illustration by Rhea-Frances Tetley.*

methods to transport materials to it. It needed tunnels and flumes to move the water. It needed excellent engineering and workers, as well as places for the workers to live and eat.

An extensive system of sixty miles of tunnels was designed to connect the lakes, instead of the initially planned canals, to eliminate the loss of water through evaporation and problems caused by ice during the winters.

The planned tunnels and dam building required heavy equipment to be brought up the mountain. The old Daley Canyon Road (built in 1870) and Devils Canyon lumber roads were considered unacceptable for this task. The original Mormon Lumber Road (1853) had gone up West Twin Creek (aka Smith) Canyon, but the route had been abandoned for over thirty-five years due to its 55 percent grades and the flooding that had washed out the road twice in the 1860s.

Also, Robert Waterman, owner of the canyon, had always opposed anyone using the Mormon Road, as he didn't want his water polluted by animals traveling along the road. When Waterman became California governor and moved to Sacramento, one of his areas of interest was clean water and irrigation.

It is believed it was Waterman's statewide water irrigation development plans that partly motivated Koebig to create the Little Bear Valley water concept. Governor Waterman left office in January 1891, when he didn't run for reelection due to poor health, and died on April 12, 1891.

ARROWHEAD RESERVOIR TOLL ROAD

The ARC decided the best route to build a new road would be up Smith (Waterman) Canyon (somewhat along the abandoned Mormon Road route) for transporting cement and equipment to the dam site in Little Bear Valley. The timing was excellent—just after Waterman's death—so it received permission from Waterman's heirs to build the road up the canyon (now renamed Waterman Canyon, as suggested by Dr. Barton of Redlands, to honor the former governor) in the summer of 1891.

The Arrowhead Reservoir Toll Road was completed in March 1892 by construction crews working seven days a week at a cost of $38,360. This made the hauling of heavy supplies to the dam construction site possible.

The lower six miles of the new road through the canyon were constructed with a fourteen-foot width, with generally an 8 percent grade and a couple of steeper grades. This was a very nice road for the era. The upper two and a half miles to the crest was routed into thirteen switchbacks carved into the ridge, with 15 percent grades and sharp curves, but it was still better than the other roads that entered the mountains at the time. The Arrowhead Reservoir Company really wanted exclusive use of the road, so it posted high toll rates.

The ARC also got county approval in 1894 to build an incline railway to bypass the sharp upper switchbacks. An incline rail system would speed the delivery of the heavy bags of cement powder for the core of the dam, since that last two and a half miles was very difficult on the animals pulling the heavy wagonloads of cement.

To haul the heavy equipment, twelve- to sixteen-horse or oxen teams were used. Since this was strenuous work, the teams needed to be rested after every mile. It would take from 4:00 a.m. to 8:00 p.m. to reach the crest, if all went well. At the crest, near Mormon Springs, the teamsters allowed the teams to rest several days before either going up to Little Bear or returning down the mountain. They usually hauled down a load of cordwood, as selling it in the valley reduced the cost of transportation, often paying for the downhill trip.

The corralled-in rest area at the crest earned the nickname by teamsters of "Fly Camp," for obvious unsanitary reasons. A bunkhouse/warehouse to protect the cement from the elements was built at Fly Camp. Years later, in 1906, a contest would be held to rename this and the nearby popular crest camping area. Dr. Wesley Thompson of Colton (later elected as the county coroner) suggested the winning name of Crestline.

The equipment and dry cement would then be hauled over to the Little Bear Valley dam site by other teams using only six to eight horses due to the lesser grades from Fly Camp to Little Bear.

When the Arrowhead Reservoir Toll Road project was completed, the heavy equipment was hauled up the mountain. Finally, in March 1892, the tunneling projects could begin. The tunnels were to connect the seven lakes by an underground valve system to control the speed of the water and maintain the lake levels.

Digging the Tunnels

The first part of the water diversion project was the Willow Creek (or Tunnel #1), begun in 1892. The tunnel was dug completely by hand power and controlled blasting. Construction started on the lakeside of the project, where Camp #1 was established for the workers to live while on the project. All the rocks removed from the tunnel—estimated at eight thousand cubic yards— were transported over to the dam site at Little Bear Creek to construct the dam.

The Little Bear Dam was initially designed to be a masonry dam, but it was discovered that the decomposed granite rock was not adequate, so it was redesigned into a cement core dam with a hydraulically compacted fill of earth on each side of it. The digging for the base of the dam was begun in 1893.

The camps for the men digging the tunnels and building the dam were adequate for their time. The workers were given free housing at the camps, sleeping on framed beds inside a tent, without plumbing or heat. They worked ten-hour days, earning forty-five cents an hour—fifteen cents more per hour than workers earned in San Bernardino at the time—and they received all the food they could eat for $1.00 a day, allowing them to net $3.50 a day.

The work on the project lasted about eight to ten months a year, depending on the weather. The meals prepared by the Chinese cooks were excellent and abundant, consisting mostly of meat, potatoes and coffee, with delicious pies for dessert. Camp #1 was the biggest construction camp and would be today located near the gatehouse of the Doheny Estate.

Tunnel #1 was initially designed to be almost 5,000 feet long with a grade of a 2-foot drop for every 1,000 feet of length, creating a gravity flow to carry water north to Willow Creek from Little Bear Basin and then west to Grass Valley. The tunnel itself is arch shaped, 6 feet wide and 7 feet tall. Where the rock was not strong enough to handle the rushing water without crumbling, the interior of the tunnel was reinforced with cement lining. The tunnel is 265 feet below Lake Arrowhead Elementary School. Tunnel #1 could handle a capacity flow of fifty thousand gallons per minute.

Inside the unused tunnel today, it is pitch black with a constant temperature in the fifties. Water seepage into the tunnel over the years has created some waterfall-looking calcium deposits coating the walls and some small

Inside the Willow Creek Tunnel in 2014, showing both the cement-sleeved walls and the rough-cut rock sides of the tunnel. *Photo by Rhea-Frances Tetley.*

stalactites an inch or more long hanging from the tunnel's ceiling. It has pipes exiting the tunnel, which were designed to provide water to the north shore homeowners in the early days. Those unused cast-iron pipes have now begun to rust.

Water seeps in and runs through the bottom of the tunnel from just a few inches deep to several feet deep into Willow Creek. All those century-old tunnels from this project are closed to the public for obvious safety reasons.

The Willow Creek Tunnel was completed and connected to the lake by way of the Outlet Tower in 1908. It is said that the outlet tower could still release the water from the lake in an emergency situation, but it would take six to nine months for the lake to totally drain exclusively through the Willow Creek Tunnel.

About 20 percent of the tunnel walls are cement lined, including the ends and where the elevator shaft connected. Tunnel #1's floor from the elevator to its exit into Willow Creek was cemented.

The tunnels were mostly hand dug by pickaxes and small tools. At first, they did not have a mechanical tunnel digger. Where the walls were not lined, all the tunnels have ragged, hand-hewn rock sides. Digging the tunnels took longer than was expected, as the rock was harder in some locations and softer than anticipated in other spots, requiring the installation of the cement liners, which put the project behind schedule.

Dynamiting, drilling, digging and tunneling through the mountain was dangerous work. Several men were injured, including one worker who was killed when a runaway debris car fell down the shaft in Tunnel #1. Tunnel #1 was the second tunnel to be completed.

The Grass Valley Tunnel #2 was designed to carry water from the Grass Valley Reservoir (now the golf course) to Meadow Bay. It is 4,172 feet long and was finished in August 1894. It was the first tunnel completed, since it faced fewer soil problems.

Tunnel C (C for "connector" tunnel) was begun near Rock Camp and was dug under current Deer Lodge Park. But the Arrowhead Reservoir Company had difficulties getting a right of way for the tunnel, which was designed to connect Tunnels #1 and #2.

When the 1893 recession hit, the Ohio investors became distressed. They had anticipated the whole project would be completed by then, with water flowing to the valley below and returning dividends on their investment. However, by 1894, the Little Bear Reservoir Project had cost $400,000, and the huge project was barely begun. Work on the Little Bear Valley Dam had not even started.

Virtually all work on the reservoir project halted when the initial $1 million funding had been spent and the few additional funds had dried up by 1897. Unpaid tunneling contractors were in court trying to get paid. Then, Colonel Adolph Wood, "human dynamo" of the entire water project, died on April 15, 1900. While taking a drive in the country, his team of horses was frightened by a metal piece of roofing flapping in the wind. The horses ran out of control; it took Wood a mile and a half to regain control. Colonel Wood, who suffered from heart problems, got out of the buggy, lay down on the grass and died from a heart attack. The future did not look promising for the Little Bear Reservoir project.

4
A Trip to Little Bear Valley in 1905

A 1905 Vacation to the Mountains

Blistering hot temperatures in the San Bernardino Valley just south of the San Bernardino Mountains are typical, with many days measuring over 110 degrees Fahrenheit. At the beginning of the twentieth century, before the advent of air conditioning, agriculture was the area's main industry. Except for irrigating groves, there wasn't much to do other than sweat. Getting away from the sizzling heat was the only way to feel cool.

Valley residents knew the Arrowhead Reservoir Toll Road, built in 1891, led up to cool breezes drifting through the tall pine trees and offered the opportunity to hunt and fish. A month-long family vacation up to the Little Bear area was a good way to escape the heat. Several families would travel and camp together, since journeying into the vast wilderness was safer in numbers. It was nearly impossible for an individual family to successfully make the trip because of the difficulties of the road and the "untamed wilderness" area they were entering.

Preparations began weeks before departure and included getting the wagon ready. First was a trip to the blacksmith shop to be sure the wheels were tight and that all needed repairs to the running gear were completed. Extra storage room and sideboards would be added on to the wagon itself, along with a spring seat.

The horses would even be given the "twice-over"—new horseshoes, baths, brushings and extra rest. All the harnesses would be repaired, cleaned and oiled. The journey and camping in the wilderness were serious undertakings.

The wagon was loaded the day before setting out with all the necessary items to sustain the family. All the clothes would be packed in a large trunk, as only emergency laundry items would be washed while they were away. This trunk was placed under the front spring seat.

A "sheet-iron stove" with an oven was brought for the cooking, in anticipation of the wild game and fish that would be eaten. The tent poles would be stored inside the stovepipe and attached to the outside of the wagon.

A mattress and springs were usually brought for the adults to sleep on, with bedrolls for the youngsters. Those large items were packed on their sides, behind the seats, along with boxes of cooking utensils, groceries, flour, rice and other necessities.

Several tents would be packed. Depending on the size of the family, up to five tents were needed for sleeping parents, girls and boys; for activities; and another for food preparation. Washtubs and washboards, buckets, lanterns, shovels, saws and axes, fishing poles and guns were all essential items to remember.

The most important item was the feed for the horses for the trip to camp and back, including a minimum of four bags of oats and barley and four bales of hay. While camping, the horses would graze in the valley near the campsite. Usually, it took two teams of horses to haul a wagon this full of gear up the steep 10 to 25 percent grade logging roads.

A quick meal would be served that morning prior to sunrise. They would meet up with the other families at the foot of the mountain at sunup. The Arrowhead Reservoir Toll Road traveled past the rebuilt Arrowhead Springs Hotel and turned into Waterman Canyon on the route to the mountains.

The first steep grade, directly west of the hotel near the entrance to Waterman Canyon, was called Chalk Grade. It took at least four horses to get over it. Those wagons with only two horses would wait until the first wagons cleared the grade, and then the horses would return to help pull the waiting wagons. This was the first of many good reasons to travel as a group.

After all the wagons had cleared Chalk Grade, they would reach the tollhouse and gate after about four hours of travel. San Bernardino County had purchased the Arrowhead Reservoir Toll Road and had made it into a public road by this year (1905), so no toll was due. As the wagons continued their slow trek upward, there were several watering troughs in Waterman Canyon along the road that had been set up by the Arrowhead Reservoir

A wagon driver with a whip traveling the Arrowhead Reservoir Road up Waterman Canyon, circa 1906. *Photo by Steele; author's collection.*

Company for its horses and oxen. The older children usually walked alongside the wagons. The caravan of wagons would stop at each water trough to rest the horses.

Most travelers stopped at every trough for a short while and lingered at the last watering trough at the top of the canyon, after about ten hours of travel. There, just past the Vail Ranch, the horses would be unhitched, fed, given some more water and allowed to rest. The kids would gather up firewood, and a light supper would be made. After a couple of hours of rest, the trip would be resumed.

It was now dark, and the older children would be given lanterns and told to walk ahead of the wagons to both light the way and warn downhill wagons of the uphill wagons. This narrow one-lane section of road was known as "the switchbacks," and because of the lack of trees over the roadway, it was good to travel that section of road in the coolness of night. The switchbacks went back and forth from the top of Waterman Canyon all the way to the crest.

When the kids heard bells, it meant a heavily laden lumber wagon was on its way downhill. One of the kids would run back to the uphill-bound wagons and warn them to get into a wide spot, as the downhill wagons had right of way. The remaining children would wave their lanterns and inform the lumber wagon drivers of the uphill traffic.

Several stops were planned along the switchbacks, some for the view and others to rest and feed the horse teams. Laurel Turn and Panorama Point were favorite spots to rest, and everyone stopped at Oak Flat, as it preceded the last big grade before Fly Camp would be reached. This grade again required at least four horses to pull the wagon.

By the time Fly Camp was reached, it was seven o'clock on the second morning. Most everyone stopped at the crest, as there were more water troughs and shade, an area to feed horses and a place to serve breakfast just past the crest, near the cool creek at Mormon Springs.

The name Fly Camp, although not appealing, was a legitimately earned moniker because that's where the Arrowhead Reservoir Company had its corrals for resting the oxen and horses that hauled the bags of cement up the mountainside for the dam it was building in Little Bear Valley. It was named for the hordes of flies that found the corrals to their liking.

After breakfast, the children would again walk alongside and in front of the wagon as they continued along their way, doing things kids do, such as throwing rocks at moving things like squirrels, birds and lizards. After leaving Fly Camp (which was renamed Crestline in 1906), the grade was strenuous until Camp Skyland was reached. By 1905, there were already a few private summer homes in the area that had been enjoyed by campers since the 1890s. The Skyland Inn opened in 1905 and became quite a popular resort.

When the road met the rim just before the Squirrel Inn, travelers would rest and enjoy the view out to the ocean, which from Sphinx Rock was magnificent. The streets and many buildings in San Bernardino could be seen, and the landmarks of Colton and Rialto, especially Slover Mountain, were easily identifiable.

If their arrival was around sunset, the oranges and pinks of the sunset sky reflecting on the distant ocean were to be spoken about for years, and the many buildings with lights being turned on would look almost magical.

The road then veered into the forest, going past the Squirrel Inn, an exclusive private club for the wealthy, and Pinecrest, a camping resort about to open to the public.

The wagons slowly passed the summer community of tent cabins at Strawberry Flats, including the cabin of the "Scot Bard of the mountains, Uncle Billy Stephens." There was another watering trough there, and after another rest, the journey continued.

The horse-drawn wagons traveled carefully down the long, rutted Applewhite Grade, which had been a heavily used lumber route into Blue Jay Canyon, finally reaching lower Kuffel Canyon by late afternoon. Their intended camping destination was a flat-floored canyon area with a stream and spring not far away and a meadow for the horses to graze. It was a very beautiful area to camp.

If all had gone correctly, they arrived in the late afternoon and quickly set up their tents before it got dark. Essentials were removed from the wagon before taking a well-deserved night of rest after almost forty hours of travel.

The next morning, the men would take one wagon to the sawmill to get boards to make floors and walls for some of the tents. A little community was being created that would last for several weeks; the hope was to stay long enough to outlast the sizzling heat in the valley below.

By the time all the tents had been fully erected and everything put into its place, it was almost nightfall again. The younger children spent that first day collecting firewood for the steel cook stove, with the older ones collecting logs for the big campfire for the evening—chores the kids would be expected to do daily.

The men planned to do the hunting for the meat for their families. A deer could provide food for everyone for several days and then be dried into jerky for later. Hunting trips would take the men away for several days, so they took the horses to get deeper into the forest.

Fishing was the other way to get "free" food, and the older kids could spend the days away from the watchful eyes of the adults at camp if they went fishing a mile or so from the campsite. The older boys would usually spend their days hiking in the forest, often going down to the sawmills to watch the lumbermen clear the land that would someday be under the water of the future lake. Sliding down the sawdust piles could easily fill an entire afternoon with fun.

After supper was the best time of the day for the families. The big evening campfire would be lit, and everyone would sit on logs or rocks while songs were sung. Often, the children would perform skits.

Sometimes, the adults would share their family's story of getting to California, as told to them by their parents. This was a time when family heritage was passed down from generation to generation.

Sometimes, "Uncle Billy" Stephens himself would stop by to entertain the campers. He usually arrived at dinnertime and would stay afterward to entertain. Uncle Billy traveled all over the west end mountaintop area, entertaining campers with his concertina, wild stories and singing. Another frequent camp visitor during those days was John Brown Jr., who would tell stories about fighting bears and Indians, which scared the children, but it was said they never wanted him to stop for fear they'd miss something exciting.

Those summer days were spent learning about the plants and animals and how to survive in the wilderness, performing chores to sustain the group and relaxing—a rare pleasure for that era.

After several weeks, everything they brought with them would need to be packed back into the wagons, and the return trip down the mountain began. The return trip took almost as long as the uphill trip, and the danger of a runaway wagon was ever present.

Despite what we today would consider many inconveniences, the trip to the mountains up and down the dusty roads and the days in between were considered great adventures and delightful vacations.

5

The Twentieth Century Begins and So Does Dam Construction

JAMES MOONEY GETS INVOLVED

A member of the Arrowhead Reservoir Company board, James Mooney, journeyed from Ohio in 1902 to oversee the stalled investment. After the death of Colonel A.H. Wood in 1900, the work on the project had stopped. Mooney infused $1 million of his own funds to jump-start the project. After ten years of construction, the Lake Arrowhead Reservoir project was over budget and out of funding, and construction had not even started on one of the dams.

Construction began again in 1902 after a hiatus on the whole seven-lake project. E.H. "Ted" Kellogg was the new planning engineer, replacing Koebig. Kellogg had many good ideas and motivated his workers to complete the work in a quick and efficient manner. Unfortunately, expediency often led to the job not being done correctly, so Kellogg spent much of his time trying to correct mistakes.

Kellogg actively sought out the heavy equipment needed for the large project from as far away as San Francisco. A narrow-gauge rail system, one steam locomotive and another locomotive called Black Annie, along with forty-five dump cars and four miles of railroad tracks, all had to be brought up the dirt road through the Waterman Canyon switchbacks and over to the Little Bear Dam site by slow animal power.

In 1902, the Hesperia Land and Water Company filed the first of several lawsuits against the Arrowhead Reservoir Company, complaining about the

Building the base and cement core of Arrowhead Dam. *Author's collection.*

potential loss of water that would otherwise naturally flow to their area if not diverted to San Bernardino for irrigation purposes.

To capture enough water for the seven-lake project, more inlet shafts were bored. The new completion date predicted that water would reach San Bernardino by 1908.

A new fifteen-thousand-foot-long (2.8 mile) tunnel from Deep Creek had a nineteen-person crew working on the tunnel. Due to difficulties, however, only two miles of that tunnel were ever completed.

New water collection tunnels and shafts were dug in the Sheep and Shake Creek areas to direct water to the Hook Creek water flume to send water to the new lake. The 3,312-foot-long Hook Creek Tunnel (0.6 miles long) was dug with a 9-foot diameter and completed to empty into Emerald Bay. More tunnels, shafts and flumes were planned and started to connect all of the lakes.

In 1904, Tunnel #2 was having cave-in problems, slowing down its extension toward Grass Valley and its connection with Tunnel C. The mountain's rock was found to be inappropriate for tunnels. Either the rock was too soft and

In 1926, Flora Schmitz, Lural Mills (Schafer), Don Schafer and Owen Mills sit on one of the old Shay engines used to haul dirt and rocks to build the dam. Brought around the horn on a Windjammer to California, it was one of the first locomotives on the Pacific Coast, initially operating between downtown San Francisco and the Cliff House. It was on display in Lake Arrowhead Village through the 1940s, when it was scrapped for the war effort. *Photograph by Lural Schafer; author's collection.*

needed cement liners to stop the cave-ins or it was so hard that it took a long time to dig through it. Only six and a half miles of the proposed sixty miles of tunnels of the massive project were ever completed.

By 1904, Little Bear Valley had been finally cleared of the remaining trees, and the footings were excavated forty feet down for construction of the dam. The decomposed granite rock in the area was found to be too unstable for a masonry dam to be built.

It was then decided that a cement-core, earthen-filled dam would work. The base would be 60 feet thick, and it was designed to be 114 feet tall. Little Bear Creek was diverted, and construction began late in 1904, despite the lawsuit that had been filed by the Hesperia Land and Water Company protesting the diversion of the natural flow of water from its side of the mountain.

The reservoir project was refinanced to $6 million and renamed the Arrowhead Reservoir and Power Company (AR&PC), as the Ohio investors had decided to also build powerhouses to generate electricity from the water moving through the tunnels and flumes. The new incorporation papers were filed in Wilmington, Delaware. The officers of the new corporation retained many of the former investors. James N. Gamble was president, and Benjamin F. Ehrman was secretary, with James E. Mooney, C.A. Gordon, H.H. Bechtel, James E. Brown and C.B. Mathews as directors.

More equipment was purchased, including a steam hammer, a saddleback and steam shovels, all of which were hauled up the dirt roadway to the growing dam by fourteen-horse teams and lots of block, tackle, rollers and cribbing by labor crews. By the end of 1905, the cement core wall of the dam was forty-three feet tall.

CONSTRUCTION OF THE INCLINE RAILROAD

In 1905, the Arrowhead Reservoir Company Toll Road was purchased by San Bernardino County (against the wishes of the AR&PC) and became a free county road, resulting in traffic doubling. The AR&PC sought new, faster means to transport the cement to the crest instead of the sixteen-hour horse-drawn wagon trips.

The decision was made to quickly build a cable car to haul up the heavy cement, since approval had been granted in 1894. James Mooney had used such cable systems in Ohio to transport raw goods and people up inclines. Known as the Incline Railroad, the rail cars loaded with cement were to be pulled up the forty-five-degree grade of the mountain by a steam-powered wench engine at the top of the mountain. There would be two rail cars that would counterbalance each other as they went up and down the rail line. Mooney saw this as a modern solution to their long-term cement delivery system, since cement was required for lining the tunnels, the outlet tower and now the dam's core.

Beginning in December 1905, the railroad bed for the incline was cut in from upper Waterman Canyon to Skyland by a grading crew. Skyland was a popular camping area and front cliff location directly north of the end of the 8 percent grade part of the road in upper Waterman Canyon. The design by dam project engineer Kellogg had been carefully drawn so the trestles and rails could be preconstructed off-site and brought in and laid quickly.

The track-installing crews began laying track on May 1, 1906. The crew was on schedule, laying one hundred feet of track a day. The prefabricated assemblies of rails and ties were attached vertically to the front of the work car and then pulled up the grade by the donkey steam engine and installed.

All was going well and on schedule, with about two-thirds of the track laid, when a huge thunderstorm hit in June, washing away 150 feet of the graded rail bed. When the ground dried, the rail-laying crews continued their job, not realizing that the changed grade through the washed-out area would result in a dip in the alignment of the rails. They were on a tight schedule because the cement was needed as the dam rose in Little Bear Valley.

The incline was promptly completed, and the first shipment of three tons of cement was sent on July 31, 1906. The bags of cement were being "inclined" up the mountain until they reached the dip. The incline car suddenly jumped from the tracks, dumping its load due to the long cables and the dip in the tracks. Workers reloaded the bags, and they were delivered to the top, where the waiting teamsters took them by wagon to the dam construction site, as planned.

Problems with the incline continued. The cables got snagged on the cross ties above the dip and cut into them. Different loading methods were tried, but the counterbalancing design of the cars, compounded with the dip, resulted in many tons of cement going back down the mountain to keep the cars balanced and on the tracks.

Engineer Kellogg wanted the system to work, so he designed a system of catches and carriers, attempting to hold the cars on the tracks. He even changed to an electric-powered engine for smoother power. Next, he tried cutting the huge cable into pieces and soldering them together. None of the fixes worked. After over a year of frustration, the Incline Railroad was abandoned.

Looking down the Incline Railroad tracks in 1907. *Author's collection.*

The initial rush to complete the incline was the flaw that led to its demise, resulting in the tons of cement continuing to be delivered slowly by animal power.

In July 1911, on the railroad's five-year anniversary, a huge fire swept through Waterman Canyon, destroying all the incline's wooden ties and trestles. It was a sad demise to an idea that would have modernized access to the mountains forever; instead, haste meant waste.

THE OUTLET TOWER

On September 19, 1907, a contract was signed for a unique outlet system to be built at the portal of Tunnel #1 to allow water to flow into Willow Creek. The tower would be a deep-based, poured concrete cylinder release tower that would allow control and aeration of the water released from the lake. The walls were two feet thick, with screens and valves to control the flow of water out of the lake and into the Willow Creek Tunnel. The contract was given to Arthur S. Bent, a Los Angeles contractor, who immediately began work on the tower. By the end of 1907, the Little Bear Dam was ninety feet tall.

Water was (after seventeen years of planning and building) beginning to fill the Little Bear Valley, creating a water reservoir. As the water level rose, the cement-core wall of the dam began to bulge and leak. This was a disaster. The lake level had to be lowered, while Chief Engineer Kellogg

A steam shovel working on dam construction. *Author's collection.*

tried numerous fixes. It seemed Kellogg always had to fix everything after it was built, and then it still didn't work properly. When none of his retrofitting attempts solved the leaking problem, in January 1908, when the tower was about half complete, Kellogg resigned.

The outlet tower was built in bedrock on a 6-foot slab set on a 31-foot square. It was 17 feet across at the base, which tapered at the 109-foot level to

The completed outlet tower that connected to the Willow Creek Tunnel, designed to release water to go to San Bernardino for irrigation purposes. *Author's collection.*

walls of fifteen inches thick, with a diameter of 13 feet. It had a vertical ladder down the interior so engineers could climb down to manually operate the doors to the inlets. It connected to the tunnel by a concrete elbow.

The outlet tower was finished, complete with precast brackets for an outside ladder to reach the control room located at the top of the tower.

As the water inlet to Tunnel #1, the tower worked as designed. To turn on the machinery at the outlet tower, someone would row out and climb up the ladder to the control room. This resulted in less water flowing downstream to Hesperia. The lawsuits from the Hesperia Land and Water Company got more intense, with their belief that it was a theft of their water. In response, the AR&PC purchased all the downstream land they could, including the Las Flores Ranch, trying to mute Hesperia's water rights claims.

Arthur Bent formally presented the 189-foot-tall outlet tower to the Arrowhead Reservoir and Power Company on Sunday, July 5, 1908.

In 1914, Frank Mooney, financier James Edgar Mooney's nephew, installed a standby generator at the bottom of the gate shaft, which was operated by the electricity generated by the rushing tunnel water. To turn it on, someone had to be lowered by the steam hoist in a bucket down the 185-foot shaft, which was better than the ladder originally used.

The outlet tower generated electricity for north shore homeowners. The AR&PC claimed in 1917 that it had the capacity to generate $300,000 worth of electricity a year.

In 1927, the outlet tower was used after a nine-inch rain melted a foot of snow, allowing water to flow to Willow Creek and avert a flood.

In 1929, the Lake Arrowhead utility sold all its assets to Southern California Edison, ending the outlet tower's generation of electricity for the area.

The completion of the tower was a real achievement. One hundred years later, on July 5, 2008, the outlet tower was given a 100th birthday party by the Arrowhead Lake Association and designated Cultural Landmark #8 by the Rim of the World Historical Society. Cupcakes and key chains were given to all boaters and kayakers who "met at the tower" for the party.

Today, a small elevator capable of holding two or three people operates inside the tower. The elevator was visited on camera by *California's Gold*'s Huell Howser, but the vertical ladder remains just in case.

DRIVING TO LITTLE BEAR IN 1909

The winter of 1908–9 started out with a foot of snow in December and then seven inches of rain on January 21, with snowfall after snowfall for weeks afterward.

In 1909, in Redlands, two hundred families already owned automobiles. This information encouraged Dr. John Baylis, owner of the new Pinecrest Resort in Twin Peaks, to petition the board of supervisors on April 26 to open the county-owned Arrowhead Road to automobile traffic certain days of the week. To persuade them completely, his petition included an invitation to drive the route, which was immediately accepted.

With three officials (and a driver and mechanic) in each of the seven cars, the supervisors left San Bernardino City Hall at 7:30 a.m. on April 28, following Little Bear Dam contractor Andrew Drew's Oldsmobile. He usually drove the formerly private Arrowhead Reservoir Road to the dam project about four times a month. Unfortunately, April 28 was foggy, with only forty-foot visibility, so the fabulous valley views advertised by Baylis had to be imagined.

The autos that followed Drew's Oldsmobile were a Packard, a Stanley Steamer, a Northern, a two-cylinder Reo, a Stevens Duryea and a Tourist. The cars passed several horse-drawn wagons along the road, but none of the animals was spooked, and the motorized vehicles were able to ascend the grade easily. All arrived safely up the mountain, except for the Northern, carrying Senator Willis, which broke down at the head of Waterman Canyon.

They arrived at the north end of the dam at 11:00 a.m. The men swarmed the cement mixers, steam shovels, locomotives and other construction equipment at the site. They saw the 195-foot-tall outlet tower that had been dedicated the previous July and were told of the 1,100-foot-long tunnel below it, running out to Willow Creek, designed to transport the water to San Bernardino.

The officials were treated to a luncheon delight of "beef à la mode" with brown gravy, mashed potatoes, stewed corn, lima beans and homemade bread and butter topped off with pie.

The officials were greatly impressed by the journey, the food and even the beautiful, smiling waitresses who served the delicious meal. The visitors hoped the Little Bear workers were regularly treated to similar meals.

The auto trip worked. Four days later, the supervisors voted to open the Arrowhead Road to personal automobile traffic, beginning on May 15. Autos could go up the mountain on Wednesdays from noon to midnight

LAKE ARROWHEAD CHRONICLES

and from noon on Saturdays to noon on Sundays. To eliminate the possibility of head-on collisions, downhill traffic was restricted to from noon on Sundays to noon on Mondays. However, automobile traffic was limited to well-graded roads.

With the reality of motorized travel to the San Bernardino Mountains, fishermen, tourists, campers and others could visit the mountains more easily. Fishermen flocked to the creeks, and as the Little Bear Dam was nearing completion, they were eyeing the location of the future lake with great anticipation because the roads leading there were good. Camping and fishing became so popular that the local game warden had to stop poaching and enforce each fisherman's fifty-trout-per-day limit taken out of Little Bear Creek near Camp Blue Jay. The Fish and Game Association stocked the streams and imported grouse and wild turkeys for the fishermen and hunters.

The California Supreme Court's Miller-Lux decision in 1908 had upheld the riparian right doctrine, under which the Hesperia Water Company was suing. The first lawsuit filed by the Hesperia Land and Water Company had been filed against the AR&PC in 1902. This worried AR&PC officials but did not deter them from continuing to build the Little Bear Dam.

To support its own riparian claim to the flow of water, the AR&PC, in January 1909, purchased the Las Flores Ranch and tried to get its hands on all the land it could to support its claim to the water. The AR&PC continued to add to the height of Little Bear Dam, which was nearing completion, and began to drill a whole new tunnel system on Shake and Sheep Creeks to bring more water from behind Heap's Peak into its system.

The AR&PC brought in the most modern electric-powered air compressor drilling equipment for the Deep Creek Tunnel. It surveyed and then hung electrical wires from the head of the Incline Railroad (Skyland) across Huston and Wixom flats to the dam site and beyond to power the new machinery.

Army engineer Perry Green came to visit his brother, Max, at the Little Bear Commissary. Perry saw the boxes of air compressor equipment, exactly like those he had worked on at Fort Yuma. No one locally knew how to assemble the compressor equipment, which was being stored at the Sheep Creek Tunnel site, out of the elements. Perry was hired and moved into the bunkhouse.

The end of 1909 saw the AR&PC closing up most of its operations for the year. This included rounding up the cattle, halting the delivery of cement to the dam site and rearranging the earth-filling equipment as the dam's core wall grew. Work on the dam continued until the first week of December, when it snowed, sending most of the workers, including the machinists, laborers and cooks, home for the winter. This left only a few caretakers, including Max and Perry Green, at the dam site, with guns to shoot ducks for meat and fish. With some supplies to last the winter, they figured they would be just fine spending their first winter on "the Heights."

The Green brothers went on to work for Kirk Phillips in 1912 and, after Phillips's death, became the owners of Mountain Auto Line in 1914. Mountain Auto Line transported most of the vacationers up and brought supplies to the year-round residents in the San Bernardino Mountains until the Greens sold the company in 1931 to Pacific Electric Motor Transit System, where they were hired on as managers.

1910, A YEAR OF GREAT CHANGES

The first part of 1910 brought rain and snowfall so heavy that it even stalled the trains in the Cajon Pass due to debris slides and the washing out of the tracks. By April, the snows had melted enough, but no one returned to work at the Little Bear Dam site, and the problems from the lawsuits claiming water rights to the AR&PC basin had to be resolved.

In May, big problems were found at the dam site. Several less-than-one-inch-wide cracks were discovered through the core wall, and the wall was bulging out a foot from the weight of the water filling up the lake.

On May 6, Engineer Walter Hy Brown and his assistant, James Valentine, quit due to Brown's deep dissatisfaction with consulting AR&PC engineers Finkle and Trask, who were recommending what he considered inadequate repairs to the core wall. They had recommended releasing just six to twelve inches of water daily through the new outlet tunnel into the Willow Creek Tunnel, and then some remedial action would be considered. Brown said, "I am not willing to risk my integrity as an engineer in its application."

Brown had hired another engineer to try to figure out a solution. Brown's engineer stated that the reason for the leakage was "the poor quality and shattered condition of the rocks upon which the dam was built, not from any failure of Brown's work…A slip in the earth's crust [an earthquake?] caused the wall also to be thrown out of line."

Contractor Arthur Drew said he would make the AR&PC's recommended repairs but refused to be held liable if they didn't work after he had followed its recommendations. Drew sent his thirty men, wagons, teams and a steam

Right: Building the cement core at the center of the earth-filled dam; notice the engines dumping carfuls of dirt on each side of the cement core wall. *Author's collection.*

Below: Drew Construction's steam shovel up close. This had to be hauled up the mountain by oxen power. *Author's collection.*

shovel to begin work. In the meantime, the lawyers began to square off in court in San Bernardino.

In May 1910, AR&PC director James Mooney sent his secretary, C.A. Gordon, out from Cincinnati as Walter Hy Brown arrived with his lawyers and witnesses to complete a transfer of management from Brown to repair the cracks found in the earth-filled dam.

Drew's contract and all his equipment were purchased for $50,000, and he was freed from future penalties for lack of completion. F.E. Trask was appointed chief engineer for the AR&PC. After a complete inspection, it was determined that the "temperature cracks will not vitally affect the integrity of the wall." A new foreman, W.J. Blair, was selected by the AR&PC to continue the dam work, and workmen began to arrive by way of the Lyman Stage Company by July.

The *San Bernardino Sun* wrote on August 3, 1910:

Load after load of long, twisted steel rods are being hauled up the Arrowhead Grade into Little Bear Valley to be used in reinforcing of its big dam there. A curtain wall is to be carried…beyond the point where the cracks developed, clear across the lower side of the core wall toward either end, and as deep as excavation shall develop to be necessary.

The previous fall, the Arrowhead Reservoir and Power Company had cut trees for power transmission lines, creating a fire danger with the downed wood and debris left behind.

Frank Mooney, Director James Edgar Mooney's nephew and a recent graduate from an Indiana engineering college, came to observe the progress on the leaking dam repair. He directed crews as they strung transmission wire from the incline in Skyland along the AR&PC's right of way to the dam site, this time cleaning the debris as they went. The timbers used to build the frame towers for the span across Grass Valley were from the company's sawmill, now managed by Henry Guernsey.

Mooney rode out daily to the work site, where the work crew, with a chuck wagon and all its work gear, was camped. Mooney stayed at the AR&PC's gatehouse and commissary with Max and Perry Green, who were hauling food between Tunnel Camps #1 and #2 that summer. Eighteen teamsters, including Mr. Knight, Bemis, Newcombe and the Wixom brothers, delivered freight to the AR&PC, and beginning on October 7, a Mr. Freeman was hired to drive a motorized wagon.

In September, the summer grazing cattle at Little Bear Valley were herded down the dusty, rocky, Waterman Canyon Road to market by vaqueros from the Los Flores Ranch. The forest rangers were busy harvesting cones from the Jeffrey and sugar pine trees. The dried cones produced hundreds of pounds of seeds for future reforestation projects. The rangers reported, "The acorn crop was large enough to fatten a million hogs." So John Suverkrup and his sons fenced an eighty-acre, oak tree–covered ridge on Hook Creek

Road, behind Camp Comfort on AR&PC land, in readiness for John Nish, who arrived on the mountain with a load of brood sows to spend the fall eating acorns.

Two negatives ended 1910. A fire broke out in the storehouse that was used as the sickbay, burning a worker's blanket and blistering his feet. The fire frightened everyone because it was adjacent to the hay barn and kerosene shed. Fortunately, the fire was put out before the worst occurred.

NEW LAWSUITS AND NEW DAM SOLUTIONS

In 1911, new lawsuits were filed by seventy-six landowners and Victorville's Appleton Land and Water Company claiming the right to an "uninterrupted flow of water" and further claiming that the Lake Arrowhead Reservoir and Power Company was "usurping the downstream property owner's water rights" by stealing their water. The 1908 Miller-Lux Decision in the San Joaquin Valley declared that water could not be taken from a natural watershed and diverted to another area for any purpose.

The AR&PC decided to purchase all the downstream properties along the Mojave River that it could acquire to guarantee its water rights claims. The original plan was no longer looking very profitable to the investors, as the thirty-year-old 1887 Wright Act, written while Governor Robert Waterman from San Bernardino was in office, for organizing irrigation districts and on which the Arrowhead Lakes plan was based, was now out of fashion. California, with its increasing population, had new water priorities.

Ignoring all these legal complications, new chief dam engineer F.E. Trask reinforced the core wall of the dam with heavy metal rods, and the leaking

Little Bear Valley after all the logs were removed and after the outlet tower was completed. *Author's collection.*

and bulging problems were finally solved, so water again was allowed to be stored behind the 160-foot-tall dam. The water project was now twenty years old, and the dam was only 80 percent complete. Almost $3 million had been spent, and not 1 foot of water had been delivered, with no dividends paid to the investors, who had begun selling their shares. Just to keep the project going to completion, James Mooney, now AR&PC president and chief stockholder, advanced another $1 million to complete the dam.

The original Arrowhead Reservoir plan to shift the water flow from the north side of the mountain to San Bernardino was popular when originally suggested in the 1890s, but as the water project was nearing completion in 1913, legal challenges were strongly argued.

The 1913 decision by the Superior Court in San Bernardino ended the Arrowhead Reservoir and Power Company's irrigation project dream. It would not be allowed to divert one drop of water from the desert side and could not use the $4 million it needed to complete the tunnels and other dams in the multi-lake project until clear title to the water could be proved. Since this clear title was impossible to obtain, the entire irrigation project was, so to speak, dead in the water. The tunneling and building stopped. Now what?

A fishing trip to Deep Creek—Sam Halstead, Harrison Wright, Arthur Halstead, Hutchie Colson and members of the Squirrel Inn. *Photo by Arthur Halstead, courtesy Rim of the World Historical Society.*

The Arrowhead Reservoir and Power Company had one 184-foot-tall dam, a partially filled lake, less than seven miles of tunnels, a tall water outlet tower and lots of useless property. California was a drastically different world in 1913, with electricity and automobiles, than it had been in 1891.

From the time Little Bear Lake began filling, fishermen who fished the streams leading to the lake now desired to fish in the new lake. As early as 1908, the dam construction crews had fished from the lake. In 1911, local sportsmen were also allowed to fish in the now filling lake.

James Mooney, AR&PC president, saw recreational possibilities as a way to make money from the lake. He proposed a private fishing village resort. The other investors were supportive.

6
The San Bernardino Mountains in 1914

MOUNTAINS PREPARE FOR CHANGE

The San Bernardino Mountains area was just about to change in 1914. The Crest Boulevard Wagon (and auto) Road was about to be upgraded into the Rim of the World Scenic Drive, which was designed exclusively for automobile traffic, changing travel completely. This road not only provided access but also some of the "most magnificent scenic views in the world." Those views had been inaccessible to all but those who had roughed it in wagon travel on rutted dirt wagon roads.

In 1914, the San Bernardino County Board of Supervisors announced it had just funded the building of the "New" Mountain Crest Drive, stating:

> *The road follows the crest of the mountains, reaching all the magnificent summer resorts located there. The newly named Rim of the World Drive will be open all year to vehicles. One will be able to leave San Bernardino by automobile and in an hour, traveling over this magnificent road when completed, be enjoying such vistas as can be found nowhere else in the world.*

The road was to remain open all seasons to motorized vehicles, and it was promised that the new road would change the mountain experience from that of "roughing it" to a pleasant trip that could be made by either auto stage (bus) or in a private car.

Auto stages ran daily in connection with the Pacific Electric and Santa Fe Railroads, with brochures boasting: "Tourists who have travelled the world have repeatedly stated that for grand and beautiful mountain scenery, the San Bernardino Mountains, as seen from the 'Crest Drive,' are unsurpassed. The expense of the trip is small and no visitor to California should fail to make the trip."

In 1914, the Little Bear Valley Reservoir was finally filling. The county believed that the future of the San Bernardino Valley was agriculture, with fruit tree groves and vineyards overtaking livestock and cereal and grain crops in production. San Bernardino, which had anticipated irrigating those agricultural lands, received not a drop of the impounded mountain water.

The Little Bear Valley Camp was sixteen miles north of San Bernardino, located near the campsite of the Arrowhead Reservoir and Power Company workers who were completing the dam to create Little Bear Lake. It claimed to be the oldest and finest campground in the whole San Bernardino Mountains range.

The county was developing its electrical generation capabilities, and factories were switching from steam, gasoline and water power to electricity. The Little Bear Dam had been redesigned in 1905 to also generate electricity for the area. The mountain district was only sparsely populated in 1914, and development had not been attempted, but "when the problem of transportation is solved, hundreds of pioneers may find homes in the small valleys and meadows." There were "600 acres of apple trees producing as fine apples as are grown anywhere," boasted the county.

LITTLE BEAR LAKE RESORT, 1914–1919

In 1914, the Trout Association requested permission to fish in the lake for public fishing. The request was denied. "The Arrowhead Company wishes eventually to establish a big resort on the lake...with exclusive fishing privileges," stated Mooney.

However, when the 1915 fishing season opened, the same year as the opening of the Rim of the World Highway to automobile traffic, hundreds of unwanted fishermen lined the shores of the lake, and some even launched boats. The campfires and camping around the lake greatly disturbed Little Bear Lake officials who were looking to restrict access to their lake.

The "last straw" came during a late season snowstorm, when several Little Bear Lake cabins were broken into and some fences were destroyed. On May 10, the Arrowhead Company closed the lake and charged seventy-one people with vandalism, recovering $131 from each. The fishermen threatened to sue.

A compromise was reached, allowing restricted public fishing on one and a half miles of the south shore of the lake. Gus Knight from Big Bear rented boats, and F.A. Edwards built a lunchroom and rented camping tents to the fishermen.

The next season, more than two thousand fishermen were there for 1916's opening day; however, the opening was marred when four men drowned in a boating accident. Soon, James Mooney opened a 150-bed hotel for fishermen, twenty-six rental cabins, campgrounds and a store, as the construction on the dam continued and Little Bear Lake filled.

The AR&PC began to divest itself of the extra land it owned, finally creating some funds for the investors. The value of the land had increased about 4,000 percent, partially because a lake was in the area. It sold the Huston Flats (now Lake Gregory) area to Arthur Gregory, who built a sawmill to make crates to ship the citrus fruit he grew in Redlands.

When the lake was opened to fishing in 1915, the co-owner of the hotel and dance pavilion, F.A. Edwards, applied for a post office because the nearest post office at the time was down in Skyland Heights at the top of the former Incline Railroad. A post office opened in 1916 at Twin Peaks, six

The Little Bear Resort Lake Post Office. *Author's collection.*

months before the Little Bear Post office opened in February 1917, but the Little Bear Lake application was filed first.

By 1917, there was a post office and rental cabins at the Little Bear Fishing Resort, near current-day Lake Arrowhead Village. John Suverkrup, a former lumberman, promoted Cedar Glen, overlooking the lake, as a resort and offered lots for sale. By 1918, the rustic Little Bear Fishing Resort, with its log cabins and building, was one of the most popular summertime destinations in Southern California.

By 1919, recreation was really growing around the lake. The Little Bear Resort now had a dance pavilion, twenty-six rental cabins, a restaurant, dozens of boats for rent and a 150-bed hotel. Five miles of the lakeshore were now opened to public fishing.

JAMES MOONEY SAVES LITTLE BEAR RESORT FROM RUINATION

James Edmund Mooney was one of the original Cincinnati financiers of the Little Bear Lake Dam project in 1892 and the only one who saw it through to completion. Born in 1832 in Indiana, Mooney began working at his father's leather tanning business at age thirteen, as both a salesman and as an accountant, while continuing his schooling. He saved his earnings and, after working a couple of other jobs, formed a partnership with John Clark, establishing a very successful general store.

Mooney eventually bought out the family leather business, forming new partnerships with family members while expanding its scope, and opened related companies and subsidiaries in Louisville, Kentucky, with offices in St. Louis, Chicago and Boston. He also founded the First National Bank of Columbus, Indiana. He seemed to be successful in every venture.

Mooney continued to invest. He invested in the Indianapolis water system and purchased the Muskogee Lumber Company in Florida, along with its 10,000 acres of land, which included several sawmills and railroads, expanding the owned forest acreage up to almost 100,000 acres.

Mooney moved to the center of the business world in 1875, to one of America's biggest cities—Cincinnati, Ohio—just ten years after the Civil War ended. Cincinnati had not been ravaged by the war and had become a manufacturing center in the "West" and a hub city between the North and South. "Mooney believed in the American ideal of honest hard work and personal responsibility, which were known in his day as 'industry and integrity,'" his grand nephew, James C. Mooney, told me in an interview. "My Great Uncle became involved in 1883 in Cincinnati's Mount Adams Incline and Railway Company, one of the first cable car companies in America, and later adapted this successful idea to the Little Bear Lake venture as the Incline Railroad."

Mooney also invested in the Union Gas and Electric Company of Cincinnati, one of the first electric companies in America. With that knowledge, generating electricity became part of the project at the Little Bear Dam when it recapitalized in 1906.

Overall, Mooney was involved in about fifty diverse and profitable business ventures during his lifetime.

Edward James Mooney, the man who saved the Little Bear Lake Reservoir project by creating a fishing resort. *Author's collection, donated by the Mooney family.*

As a guest speaker to the Wholesale Saddlery Association in 1889, just before he invested in the Arrowhead Reservoir Company project, Mooney expressed his opinion about America's prosperity:

> *Our boundless resources, our indomitable energy, our ingenuity and skill, our increasing population and accumulating wealth, along with the mighty developments and influences of modern civilization, have already lifted us up among the greatest national powers of the age, and are destined to make us, in the near future, the mightiest nation on the earth, and the grandest republic the world has ever known.*

When San Bernardino city engineer Adolph H. Koebig came to Ohio presenting the excellent investment opportunity of bringing irrigation water to the San Bernardino Valley, the Arrowhead Reservoir Company (ARC) was incorporated in December 1890 in Kentucky. Mooney was an original director and continued his connection with this project for thirty-five years. The ARC project became one of the largest privately funded land irrigation and water development projects ever undertaken in the United States, according to J.C. Mooney.

In 1905, the company was reincorporated as the Arrowhead Reservoir and Power Company (AR&PC). Although the project was scaled back, its new name was designed to reflect a refined purpose and direction for the now single-lake project. From Mooney's success with the incline cable systems in Ohio, he had the Incline Railroad system designed to transport the cement up the mountain and the generation of electricity added into the construction of the dam. He was a forward-looking man who incorporated new technology in his projects, which might explain why he was so successful in so many ventures.

Mooney came out to California to visit and supervise the Little Bear Reservoir project numerous times over the years, developing a special relationship with the project, despite its lack of financial return on his investment. He enjoyed the location and its peaceful surroundings, and from his cabin at the Squirrel Inn Resort, Mooney could see the island of Catalina glistening in the sun in the Pacific Ocean, over one hundred miles away.

After the 1913 landmark decision that the irrigation portion of the project could not be used, Mooney accepted the verdict, partially because of his advanced age. Mooney was in his eighties at the time, so he did not have the energy or time to fight the court decision that stopped the irrigation angle of the water project.

But that doesn't mean he gave up on the investment, as others did. James Mooney became the sole funding source, invested some more capital and developed the lake as an exclusive fishing resort, personally investing over $20 million of his own funds in the Little Bear Lake project.

He established Little Bear Lake as a prime recreational area. He then leased the boating and other concessions to local businessmen, including Gus Knight of Big Bear. In this way, Mooney created a successful recreational destination from what others considered a fiscal disaster. He sold off excess land that the AR&PC owned and created another flow of capital.

Mooney's death on September 5, 1919, in Cincinnati, Ohio, was another casualty of the great worldwide flu epidemic that swept the nation compounded by his advanced age of eighty-seven years. James Mooney, a bachelor, died without a direct descendant. His heirs in Ohio and estate administrators underappreciated the personal involvement Mooney had with the Lake Arrowhead area. His nieces and nephews saw Little Bear

Lake as a disaster of an investment and a money pit and immediately sold the "California investment." It had not brought any financial return, but it certainly provided a lot of enjoyment to Mooney.

The property was listed for $650,000, and a California investor syndicate headed by J.B. Van Nuys bought it for pennies on the dollar. But with the syndicate's twentieth-century thinking and the added investment of its capital, it created one of California's foremost and most desirable recreational destinations in the 1920s: Lake Arrowhead.

7

The Cedar Glen Story

HOOK CREEK AND CAMP COMFORT

Hook Creek runs through the community of Cedar Glen, southeast of Lake Arrowhead. Cedar Glen began as a lumber mill site, with the Hank's Mill cutting mostly pine and cedar in the area in the 1880s. The lumber was transported by horse-drawn wagons down Daley Canyon Road to be used for boxes and crates for the citrus industry.

Hook Creek flows through the 160 acres where veteran sawmill operator John Hook cut timber in his shake and fencepost sawmill in 1883. The upper stream was part of his homestead, where he built a cabin in the canyon next to the creek—thus the name Hook Creek

In 1888, Hook partnered with young John Suverkrup, and the two ran sawmills successfully together for over twenty years. They purchased two sections of trees near Deep Creek. Hook converted his circular-saw shingle mill into a lumber mill. The first year, they cut ten thousand board feet of lumber a day and expanded to cut twenty to twenty-five thousand feet of lumber a day by employing twenty men in the mill. Suverkrup opened a lumberyard in San Bernardino at the corner of F Street and First Street, selling their lumber at wholesale and retail prices. The mill operated until 1910 in the Hook Creek area.

The Arrowhead Reservoir Company established Camp Comfort in the Cedar Glen area for housing and feeding the workers on the Little Bear Dam project in the late 1890s. Deep Creek is a major waterway that feeds

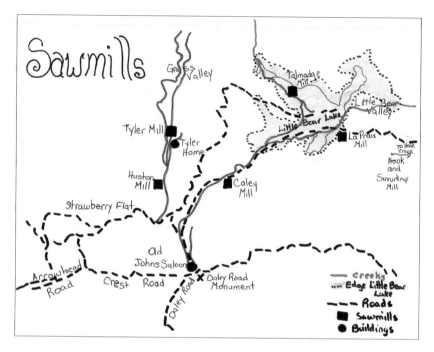

A sawmill map of the Little Bear Valley area representing mills from the 1870s to '90s. *Illustration by Rhea-Frances Tetley.*

The Hook Creek Sawmill in 1887. *Author's collection.*

into the Mojave River. Water from Deep Creek was considered an essential source for the formation of Lake Arrowhead.

The Sheep Creek area was used by the ARC to drill shafts into the ground for tunnels to collect the water. A shaft almost 13 feet in diameter was cut almost 70 feet down to the bedrock, and the lateral arch-shaped 9- by 7-foot tunnel was dug 461 feet to the east and 421 feet to the west.

A steam engine power plant was placed on a large cement slab at the top of the shaft to provide power, operating twenty-four hours a day, pumping fresh air into the tunnels and providing power for the drilling tools and the elevator platform that lowered people and materials into the tunnel. It also pumped out water that would seep into the tunnel. There were small debris cars on a rail track that brought the diggings through the tunnel to the shaft to be removed and used in the construction of the dam at Little Bear.

A second shaft at Shake Creek was 150 feet deep and was hand-dug without power tools. A lateral tunnel was built from that tunnel toward Hook Creek about one mile upstream from where the Hook Creek flume was to be built. There was a small donkey steam engine and some debris cars to remove the tailings from the tunnel.

In 1909, the refinanced Arrowhead Reservoir & Power Company (AR&PC) decided to complete the tunnel from Deep Creek and connect to the reservoir itself instead of subcontracting this tunnel. It purchased an electrically powered air compressor to speed up the digging. To power the air compressor, an electrical line was surveyed from the top of the Incline Railroad in Skyland across Wixom Flats (Blue Jay) to the dam site in Little Bear Valley. Water would be collected by seepage into the tunnels and would flow by gravity through the tunnels to the flume at Hook Creek and then into the new lake to be built at Little Bear Meadow.

Max Green (future owner of Mountain Auto Line), as a teenager, drove a supply wagon to the camps for these workers. He later shared his stories of epidemics of illness, some labor disputes and the financial difficulties the project faced over the decades of the dam project.

The biggest problem began when Congress passed the Riparian Rights Law, which forbids the diversion of water from its natural flow, which was the entire premise of the AR&PC project. It was this proposed diversion of Deep Creek water to Lake Arrowhead from its natural flow to the Mojave River that prompted the lawsuits under the new law between the desert dwellers and the Arrowhead Reservoir & Power Company. It took years, but after the AR&PC lost the lawsuit, almost immediately all of its housing camps were closed, the buildings dismantled and everything of value removed from the site.

The Sheep and Shake Creek areas returned to nature, with the shafts filling with water and being ignored. The area became part of the land purchased by the Arrowhead Lake Company but was mostly used for grazing cattle during the summer months in the early decades of the twentieth century; for hunting deer, bear and big horn sheep; and by backcountry fishermen.

Because Deep Creek is a wild trout stream, the first trout swam into Lake Arrowhead naturally as the water was diverted to fill the lake.

CEDAR GLEN

In 1910, Suverkrup bought out the older Hook Mill. The Suverkrup Mill now had rights to 640 acres in the Hook Creek area on what is now the east side of Lake Arrowhead. The mill site included a bluff area overlooking the valley being flooded for the Little Bear Reservoir. Suverkrup was the first to sell lots for vacation purposes in the Little Bear Lake area. In June 1916, Suverkrup advertised fifty-five lots "facing beautiful Little Bear Lake for sale at $150 each."

Years later, the Suverkrups' family home became the Cedar Glen Café and, later, the Sportsman Restaurant. The resort had cabins and stores for the weekenders who visited the area.

The first mail delivery to the area was by rural Star Route #3. The Cedar Glen Resort became a very popular tourist area, and residents wanted regular postal service rather than rural delivery. The first Cedar Glen Post Office was established at the Cedar Glen Resort in February 1939. The post office moved into its own building in 1962, receiving the zip code of 92321.

After World War II, Cedar Glen saw more homes built and businesses being established. The Cedar Glen (Happy Face) Malt Shop was opened in 1946, becoming a focal point of memories for mountain youth and old-timers alike for several generations.

When the Santa Anita Turf Club began donating facilities, the Los Angeles Area Council of Boy Scouts of America received a large parcel of land in the Hook Creek area for a campground. Named the Forest Lawn Scout Reservation, it is still actively used. Buildings that were burned during the 2003 Old Fire have been replaced.

Cedar Glen remained a quiet, out-of-the-way vacation spot until after the Sylmar earthquake. Lake Arrowhead's dam was declared to be vulnerable and subject to collapse if a strong quake hit, so the California Department of Safety of Dams condemned it. That's when Papoose Lake was constructed to create equal pressure on both sides of the old cement-core, earth-filled dam.

Access to the national forest and the Splinter's Cabin Trailhead is at the end of Hook Creek Road. The Pacific Crest Trail parallels fifteen miles of Deep Creek, with many wild animals inhabiting that part of the forest. Several pairs of nesting bald eagles have been sighted living year round in the Papoose Lake area adjacent to Cedar Glen.

Fisherman's Campground is located on Deep Creek about four miles east of Cedar Glen at the 5,200-foot elevation. The Pacific Crest National Scenic Trail crosses Deep Creek at the point of the Deep Creek Hot Spring. This mineral water has a constant temperature of 108 degrees. Deep Creek Lake is a naturally formed lake, located on the creek about a half mile northwest of Arrowbear Lake.

The San Bernardino County Building in Twin Peaks, built in the 1980s, used wood from Cedar Glen as its decoration, recognizing the historic value of the area.

8

The Arrowhead Lake Company Years

CONSTRUCTION OF LAKE ARROWHEAD VILLAGE

The Little Bear Fishing Resort lands were listed for sale in 1920 for $625,000.

J.B. Van Nuys (whose father developed the town of Van Nuys, California), Morgan Adams and a syndicate of investors incorporated as the Arrowhead Lake Company (ALC) and purchased Little Bear Valley Fishing Resort, lake and lands in 1921. The ALC wanted to create an upper-class resort and immediately closed the lake to the public. This came as an unwelcome surprise to fishermen because Little Bear Lake was the most popular fishing resort in Southern California at that time. The ALC's plans did not include allowing any access to its private lake. It sold off the extra lands of the AR&PC.

The Arrowhead Lake Company spent the first two years removing the rustic log buildings of the Little Bear Fishing Resort, completing the dam and building a road around the lake. The name was changed from Little Bear to Arrowhead Lake.

Van Nuys believed in Arrowhead Lake, investing $8 million in constructing a resort that would appeal to the celebrity crowd, with a French Norman/English style and themed village built to provide the necessary amenities. The ALC knew upscale visitors were anxious to escape the hustle and bustle of city living, and with the financial boom of the 1920s, they would be able to afford to experience the clean air of the forest in a refined way.

The dam, lake and outlet tower that the Van Nuys syndicate purchased in 1921. *Courtesy Dr. Don Adkins collection.*

Building Arrowhead Lake Village in 1922 with horsepower. *Author's collection.*

The early 1920s were still the era of horsepower, and horse-pulled graders leveled the land for the building of the village (front-blade bulldozers had not yet been invented).

The name "Arrowhead Lake" was chosen because of the natural Arrowhead landmark at the foot of the mountain, which was visible for miles and was very well known. The 101-mile-long Rim of the World Road accessed the Arrowhead Lake area up Waterman Canyon, going right past the Arrowhead landmark, and attaching its name indirectly to the well-known resort of Arrowhead Springs Hotel at the base of the road, the ALC believed, would aid in future advertisements.

The Arrowhead Lake Company applied to the U.S. postmaster general to change the post office's name from Little Bear Lake, but the request was denied. The post office believed the mail for the Arrowhead Springs resort at the bottom of the mountain (whose post office was established in 1887) would be confused with that for an Arrowhead Lake Post Office during sorting.

The ALC revised its name request to "Sagital" in February 1922. Sagital was a well-known Native American greeter in the vicinity. However, Van Nuys still wanted to piggyback on that Arrowhead image and wisely reversed the words "Arrowhead" and "Lake," quickly resubmitting his request before the Sagital name was approved. On April 24, 1922, the request for the name "Lake Arrowhead" was approved for U.S. Mail service, with Cephas B. Salisbury as the local postmaster. Van Nuys never changed the Arrowhead Lake Company's name to correspond to the new post office's name.

Lake Arrowhead Village officially opened on June 24, 1922, as the most modern resort in all of California. It had electric lights and other electric-powered facilities, as the finished, two-hundred-foot-tall dam generated plentiful power. Pure water was piped in from deep within the lake. At the village, there was adequate room for parking automobiles. Over $8 million was spent developing the village into the most elegant and modern resort in the San Bernardino Mountains.

Many activities were planned at the village to encourage tourists and to give "down-the-hill" people an excuse to travel up the oiled dirt mountain roads. The Rim of the World Road was planning major upgrades to make access easier. As the roads improved and car ownership increased, the number of tourists multiplied. The Mountain Stage Lines brought tourists who stayed for days in the local hotels—exactly what the ALC wanted. Long-term guests had the opportunity to enjoy the golf course, along with boating, sailing and fishing.

There were three luxurious lakefront hotel facilities to accommodate the overnight visitors. The North Shore Tavern, across the lake from the village, was accessible only by boat. It offered excellent secluded cabins. Visitors could stay one night or weeks on end away from the activities of the village area. Recreational facilities such as tennis courts, boating docks, stables and riding and hiking trails entertained the visitors. The North Shore Tavern is now the main building for the UCLA Conference Center, which is located on Tavern Bay.

The luxurious Arlington Lodge opened in 1923, situated on the beach approximately where the Lake Arrowhead Resort is now located, adjacent to the lake and village. It was later renamed the Lake Arrowhead Lodge.

Accompanied by the excellent year-round weather, positive word of mouth and the active promotion department advertising the beauty of the four seasons, Lake Arrowhead quickly became *the* popular mountain destination for Southern Californians with free time and money to spend. Dancing the evening away at the Dance Pavilion to either the Lake Arrowhead Orchestra or a special "name" band brought hundreds more weekenders to the resort. This tradition continued for decades.

There was an "exclusive club" to join for property owners and regular visitors of Arrowhead Woods. Known as the Mountain Lake Club (MLC), it had several levels of membership, including life (by application only), charter (original members), regular ($125), junior (eligible sons between the ages of eighteen and twenty-one only), social ($100) and temporary ($25 a month while being considered for membership).

Lake Arrowhead Village became a popular resort destination in the 1920s. *Author's collection.*

By 1924, the exclusive MLC had a clubhouse, a grill and card rooms for those cooler evenings spent indoors, with dormitory facilities for singles and overnight rooms for couples, located on the knoll to the west of the Lake Arrowhead Village. The club colors were brown and green, and its motto was "Happy Fugitives from the Bondage of Routine."

MLC members were actively encouraged to take advantage of the many outdoor activities such as trout fishing (both stream and lake), motor and sailboating, horseback riding (they called it "horse hiking"), golfing, tennis and skeet shooting, as well as winter sports such as ice skating, snow shoeing, skiing and sledding.

Like many of the exclusive clubs of the era, the MLC had a magazine. The *Sky-Hi* magazine described its exclusive membership in the following terms:

> *Conservatively started and well founded, the Mountain Lake Club has won a place in the class of better and finer clubs and is considered, because of its membership and government, quite exclusive. Made up of men of family and bachelors, all prominent in business and social circles throughout Southern California, the M.L.C. naturally inspires rare pride in its membership, as well as excites the envy of those desirous of becoming members.*

The economic timing for the development of Lake Arrowhead Village, resort and subdivisions was excellent. With the firm financial footing by the mid-1920s, the business climate of California was booming. People had a freedom of movement created by the automobile and the expanding state road system. Many families with discretionary funds felt secure enough to invest in vacation properties and recreation, especially since the first lakefront home sites sold for $100 each.

LAKE ARROWHEAD'S LOOKOUT TREE

The first fire lookout in the area was built in 1922, after the large Helga Fire burned from Arrowhead Springs to Deep Creek and almost to the Arrowhead Dam, consuming eighteen thousand acres. The Lake Arrowhead Corporation stationed a man on a platform during daylight hours with binoculars and a telephone, "in the highest tree [130 feet tall] on the highest peak...located approximately in the center of the property [on the North Shore]," an Arrowhead Lake promotional brochure stated. "From this

Lake Arrowhead Fire Department, 1920s. *Photo by Tony Burke; courtesy Dr. Don Adkins Collection.*

vantage point it is an easy matter to locate any fire and phone in the alarm," the brochure continued.

A fire lookout gave Lake Arrowhead property owners great peace of mind and lower fire insurance premiums, too. This lookout tree was staffed until 1934. The tree died about twenty-seven years later and was removed in 1962.

Lake Arrowhead Village was an immediate financial success. The Arrowhead Lake Company conducted an extensive publicity campaign to promote the area, using magazine articles, newspaper coverage of events and the printing of thousands of black-and-white and color postcards for visitors to send nationwide. Lake Arrowhead was considered a prestigious place to vacation.

Edi Jaun brought his love of the sport of winter skiing from Europe and taught his friends and others to ski and sled. There were tobogganing and sledding slopes and ice skating in nearby Blue Jay, and Edi would soon build a rope tow for skiing behind the school building. During the summer, he took visitors to the lake for waterskiing.

Every evening, the Lake Arrowhead Orchestra would play in the Dance Pavilion building. Over the years, the pavilion became famous for its quality entertainment, which eventually hosted well-known swing bands like the Ozzie Nelson Orchestra.

Before the lake even had water, the movie industry had come to the mountains to film silent films. The ALC encouraged the use of the varied scenery for filming. Only ninety miles from Hollywood, Lake Arrowhead had excellent hotels for stars and the crew to stay in. They had electricity, telephone service, gasoline stations and most modern conveniences in a rural setting, fulfilling the entertainment industry's requirements.

Arrowhead could look like the Alps or other places in rural Europe. The French Norman–style buildings of Lake Arrowhead Village looked European. The forest looked like the Canadian Rockies to some directors, which contrasted with the nearby badlands of the Pinnacles. The four seasons, especially with fall and the trees changing color, along with real snow and reasonably sunny weather, brought the film crews year round. These elements combined, making the Lake Arrowhead area popular with film companies from the 1920s to the 1940s.

Several areas around the lake were developed into residential and vacation chalet home sites, and there were numerous north shore estates. These developments were called Arrowhead Woods. The ALC maintained exclusive and restrictive clauses in its purchase contracts, which were common for the era. Commonly referred to today as CC&Rs, those clauses in the deeds restricted private homes from being visible from the water. Other deed restrictions regulated the minimum size of homes, required Normandy styling and dictated the location of servant entrances. Every deed restricted the excessive removal of trees.

Many movie stars, writers and directors found the seclusion and beauty of the area to their liking and built vacation homes in the Lake Arrowhead area. Myrna Loy, Buster Crabbe, Adolph Menjou and others all bought lakefront homes. The image that Lake Arrowhead had set out to create—a playground for the rich and famous—became a reality.

Beginning in 1928, the popularity of the automobile had won the hearts of Californians, so the oil-covered dirt Rim of the World Road was regraded, straightened and paved for automobile traffic. When the realigned asphalt road was completed in the 1930s, the area was ready for the traffic to increase.

DEVELOPING NEARBY TOWNS

People were living seasonally around the Lake Arrowhead area before the ALC developed Lake Arrowhead Village. Some were builders of the dam or homesteaders and ranchers, and others opened small businesses along the roadways during the Little Bear Lake Resort days of the later 1910s.

Permanent residents increased in number in the various areas after World War I, and when the roads improved in the 1920s, those people started businesses. Each small development was independently advertising to bring visitors and buyers to their resort community, competing against one another for the limited market of buyers.

As the economy of the nation grew and improved, the number of roads and cars increased, and more Californians desired to get away from the extremely hot weather of the valley. The cooler mountain climate was desirable in the 1920s before the advent of air conditioning.

BLUE JAY

When the Arrowhead Reservoir Company Road became a free public road in 1906, the area next to Little Bear Creek, which had been cut over by the Caley Sawmill, attracted many fishermen. Camp Blue Jay opened in 1907 for those who wanted to camp and fish in the mountains. The creek was filled with fish, and the daily limits of fifty trout per person were easily achieved.

Camp Blue Jay was named on August 10, 1907, for the blue, loudly squawking Steller's Jays that inhabited the area. The fishing camp remained popular until 1914.

In 1914, Art and Nora Wixom, along with their kids, homesteaded the twenty-two and a half acres from Camp Blue Jay through the canyon area, next to what would become the western shore of Little Bear Lake. Art retired as a forest ranger in 1917. On the homestead, they planted crops, raised chickens for eggs and had seven cows to supply milk at the store for the campers and local residents.

Each year, they built one additional vacation cabin. They constructed a small lake for spawning trout and a pay-to-fish pond next to Little Bear Creek. Their log cabin general store became known as "Wixom's Corner."

Since Blue Jay was at the crossroads, the Mountain Auto Stage and, later, the Pacific Electric Motor Transit line stopped at Wixom's Corner. Soon,

Wixom's Camp Blue Jay, now downtown Blue Jay. *Author's collection.*

they had thirteen rental fishing cabins, mostly built from abandoned wood from the closed Grass Valley Sawmill. The store had the first phone line in the area, which the Wixoms allowed the community to use. The first Blue Jay Post Office opened in Wixom's store on July 17, 1924, with Art Wixom serving as postmaster until 1936.

With Lake Arrowhead full of water, Blue Jay was located on the lake's shore. Blue Jay Bay was shallow and would freeze each winter, which was the beginning of the tradition of ice skating in Blue Jay. Actually, the ice skating on Blue Jay Bay was one of the many activities that the ALC advertised to lure winter visitors. The ALC needed a four-season resort to support its investment.

Stoney DeMent owned a vacation cabin in the Blue Jay area for several seasons. In 1932, the DeMent family moved full time to Blue Jay because of Stoney's poor health and his love of the area. He leased the property from the Wixoms, purchasing it in 1934, allowing the Wixoms to retire.

ALPINE/TWIN PEAKS

The area had originally been called Strawberry because of the strawberry farm, which had been homesteaded in the area in the nineteenth century. Strawberry Peak, Strawberry Flats and Strawberry Lodge all get their names from that era.

The town of Twin Peaks, begun near the Strawberry Flats Campground, is adjacent to Dr. John Baylis's Pinecrest Resort, which began in 1906 and was along the original route to Little Bear. The three brothers of the Dexter family (Greg, George and John) moved into the area separately in the later 1910s, and John built a sawmill and did winter maintenance for the Squirrel Inn resort. George ran a store, and Greg started the Alpine Terrace Resort at the crest of the former cement supply road to the Little Bear Dam area.

Twin Peaks, then called Alpine, had originally considered itself an extension of the Crestline area, as Dr. Baylis was part of the Crest Forest Resort Owners Association. Twin Peaks began its own school in 1924 at one of the cabins of the Dexter's Alpine Terrace Resort (now known as "The Antlers") with ten students. Its residents felt they were too isolated from Arrowhead to send their children to the Lake Arrowhead School and too far away from Crestline's school, located in Cedarpines Park.

ORCHARD BAY MILL AND AUTO CAMP, 1887–1920S

Orchard Bay is located on the south shore of Lake Arrowhead. Orchard Bay is named for the LaPraix's apple orchard at the location where sawmill owner William LaPraix had his Excelsior Sawmill. As mentioned earlier, LaPraix was known for planting or dropping the seeds from the apples he was always eating.

LaPraix's nephew James Fleming inherited the sawmill, land and orchard in 1887 after LaPraix died in an accident when he fell into the machinery at his mill. Fleming continued operating the mill until he sold his (renamed) Fleming Creek Sawmill to the Arrowhead Reservoir Company in 1891.

After the construction of the dam, the rising waters of Little Bear Lake created the desire for a campground for fishermen. The rising waters of the lake eventually covered most of the orchard, creating Orchard Bay.

Orchard Bay Auto Camp, 1928. *Author's collection.*

Camp Fleming at Fleming Grove on the shores of Lake Arrowhead had a lodge building with a lounge and dining room, a lobby and another lounge. The camp had separate cabins, with sleeping accommodations, for rent.

Orchard Bay Auto Camp was an improved auto camp that had spaces for about one thousand cars for fishermen; it opened in 1922. The camp had running water and sanitary facilities, cook stoves, ovens and tables for the fishermen. It had a gatehouse with a tower and strings of lights overhead. It cost one dollar a day per vehicle, which included the opportunity to pitch one tent, free firewood and use of the camp facilities. Fishing was a popular attraction at Lake Arrowhead in the 1920s. The ALC advertised that it stocked the lake with about one million fish from its fish hatchery each year.

John Muir Road runs along the shoreline of Lake Arrowhead, near Orchard Bay. It was named after the naturalist John Muir, who visited the Squirrel Inn, a private resort along the road to Little Bear Valley, in 1896, along with members of the U.S. Forest Reserve Commission to see whether the Forest Reserve concepts were working to save the forest. The devastation the sawmills had caused to the forest was quite disheartening to Muir. Most of the old-growth pine trees were gone, but the commission and Muir did see new growth of cedars, oaks, sugar pines and dogwood trees among the debris left by the lumbermen. This street was named in honor of John Muir's visit to the mountains and his efforts to preserve the forest.

In the early 2000s, additional apple trees were planted in the shore area of Orchard Bay, and picnic tables were added. The walking trail around the lake goes through the new apple tree orchard, reviving the historical name for the area.

SKYFOREST

The community of Skyforest (originally called Forest in the Sky) began when the Joseph Henck family became the property managers for the new development, which they began in 1923. It was created from the old Kuffel homestead established in 1889. The Rim of the World Road was cut through this land in 1915. After World War I, many owners of private land began to subdivide their property to make lots available for vacation homes. Mary Putnam Henck, Joe's wife, had been a schoolteacher and vice principal in Los Angeles for twenty years. She also had been an early organizer of the Ramona Pageant in Hemet, so she was used to creating and organizing large events. She wanted her children to attend school locally, so she found thirteen children of school age and organized the parents from Cedar Glen to Blue Jay to request a school for the mountains. She suggested to the county that it open a school, but officials told her if she wanted one to organize it herself.

She asked J.B. Van Nuys, the owner of the Arrowhead Lake Company, for help in finding a location for a school. He offered a three-room building for the school to use during the non-summer months. The storefront building was just north of the village Dance Pavilion and was used by a doctor during the summer months. A pot-bellied wood-burning stove provided heat.

The school opened for students on September 22, 1924. The county provided books, paper goods and desks. The Lake Arrowhead School opened with thirteen children, but as the news got out, it quickly grew to twenty-five students. When the weather got colder, the student attendance numbers went down again, as most students walked to school.

Almost immediately, more classroom space was needed for grades first through eighth. The Arrowhead Lake Company donated land for a school building just outside the village. At the personal urging of Mary Henck, the parents passed a $40,000 school bond, and a new building was constructed.

The first Lake Arrowhead School, now San Bernardino County Fire Station No. 91.
Author's collection.

The school opened with forty-three students enrolled and two teachers on September 20 for the 1926–27 school year.

The first Lake Arrowhead district school board had three members, and Alpine (Twin Peaks) residents were finally convinced to send their children to the new Lake Arrowhead School after John Dexter joined the school board and a school bus was purchased to transport students to the new school site.

The new school building had four main rooms, restrooms, an office, utility rooms and an upstairs assembly room. There was a real furnace located in the basement. The Lake Arrowhead San Bernardino County Fire Department now uses the two-story building as Fire Station No. 91.

Cedar Glen, Twin Peaks, Skyforest, Arrowhead Woods and Blue Jay sent children to the new school and discovered that it became the uniting element that coordinated the Arrowhead communities into working together with a common interest: educating their children.

The 1928–33 realignment of the Rim of the World Road, with the elimination of the switchbacks and the new section of road cut into the southern face of the mountain (the Narrows), made it possible to drive directly to Lake Arrowhead. Lake Arrowhead continued to promote itself as an "upscale, four-season lakeside resort" but now with easy auto access along the beautiful "Rim of the World High Gear Road" advertising many recreational activities nearby.

When the stock market crashed on October 29, 1929, the well-financed Lake Arrowhead Village was a successful resort and growing community. The village had markets, stores, automotive facilities, a school with over forty students and more than 125 water connections, with additional property around the lake for sale. It continued to advertise the nine-hole golf course, nightly dancing in the pavilion, fishing and boating, hiking and snow activities. Lake Arrowhead had everything the affluent Roaring Twenties person could want, plus the area was not as "dry" as demanded by the Eighteenth Amendment (Prohibition), ratified in 1920. Those who still had money continued to visit the lakefront resort.

PROHIBITION

The bootleggers of the Prohibition era found the isolation of the mountains appealing, too. Worthington Squint, of Squint's Ranch on the north side of Arrowhead, was allegedly a bootlegger who supplied many locals, restaurants, clubs and visitors with the illegal hard stuff, making him a popular figure in the area. He was never convicted of bootlegging.

Some even claim that Arrowhead Villas had a still that created the purest of distilled liquid. It is believed and somewhat documented that movie stars, such as Jack Benny, would drive up to vacation in Lake Arrowhead, party at the lake and then fill their "second gas tanks" with the high-quality "white lightning" before they left for home.

This all led to a positive cash flow for the local community. It is even said some local children (and therefore their families) benefitted, as they were paid to be on the lookout for the "Prohibition enforcers" and to sound the warning when they saw the government vehicle caravan driving up the mountain roads to perform a raid. This early warning system gave the drinkers and gamblers time to "clean up their acts" before the raids.

1923–1929: TONY BURKE

In his 1978 book, *Palm Springs, Why I love You*, former Englishman Tony Burke, who, among other things, was a stage actor, became an early resident of Lake Arrowhead. He recalled an incident that occurred at the mile-high resort in the early 1920s. While working in Hollywood selling radios, he was sent to the mountains to install an expensive "Superhexteradyne" radio at the vacation home of a wealthy banker. After he installed the radio unit, Burke fell in love with the tranquility of the forested area, and when the banker gave Burke a boat tour of Lake Arrowhead, he promised himself to return soon.

Working in Hollywood for MGM on the production end of the movie business, Burke soon looked up the Arrowhead Lake Company, landing a job selling real estate for it, and within a week, he was in Lake Arrowhead, working in the sales office. He was an affable man who made friends easily. But Hollywood and acting never left his mind, and he soon met the cast members—including Edward Everett Horton, Lionel Belmore and director Wallace Worsley—who were staying at the Lake Arrowhead Lodge while filming the Paramount movie *The Man Who Fights Alone*. They got along so well that they invited him to play billiards.

A movie crew filming at Lake Arrowhead during the silent era. *Author's collection, donated by Lee Cozad.*

When Burke arrived, the hotel owner led them beyond the billiard room, through a small obscure door, up a steep flight of steps and through a trapdoor into a room just under the roof. It was a large room set up, as he described, as a "gambling den, with three sharply dressed croupiers in dinner jackets." In the room were a roulette table, craps and blackjack tables and other gaming devices. "I had never seen such a place except on the screen," Burke wrote. Drinks were offered all around (despite the Prohibition laws), and the actors got down to business at the gaming tables. Horton had quite a pile of chips in front of him, Burke recalled. Burke also began betting, won a little and was enjoying it—until the trapdoor opened and two large men with guns entered the room, pointing the weapons at the gamblers and demanding that they not move. Of course, everyone froze in his or her seat and was only slightly relieved when the men identified themselves as the law.

The San Bernardino sheriff's deputies placed the croupiers under arrest and searched the room for hidden cheating wires, though none was found, and then they removed all the gambling cloths and chips, taking them with them as they went down the stairs. The event sent shivers through Burke, but none of the gamblers was arrested. The hotel manager made bail for the croupiers, and all the confiscated money was "made good" the following day to cover the gamblers' losses.

Burke continued to live in Lake Arrowhead, selling homes to many actors, including Rod La Rocque and Hungarian actress Vilma Banky, and meeting pilot Amelia Earhart. He was invited in the fall of 1929 to sell real estate that winter in Palm Springs. He did and became a great publicist and photographer for that desert resort community, never to return to live in Lake Arrowhead.

LAKE ARROWHEAD'S WATER QUESTIONS ANSWERED, 1929 STYLE

In the 1929 brochure *Smart Facts About Lake Arrowhead*, questions were answered to lure potential land buyers to Lake Arrowhead instead of to other mountain communities during the boom era before the Great Depression.

In the very beginning of Lake Arrowhead Village, it was decided by the Arrowhead Lake Company (ALC) that Lake Arrowhead should never be the ordinary type of mountain resort, so it built a European-style resort and village and required all future buildings constructed on the ALC property to be approved by the architectural committee to maintain property values and guarantee high-quality construction in its upscale development.

Since Lake Arrowhead was a private lake and the site occupied by the lake and the dam, along with the 5,000 acres entirely surrounding the lake, were all owned by the Arrowhead Lake Company, it could extend special advantages and exclusive privileges to property owners, such as boating, bathing, fishing and lake usage rights. Lake Arrowhead is 160 feet deep and covers 775 acres with a capacity of 47,000-acre feet. Its shoreline is fourteen miles long.

Advertising of the era boasted:

Lake Arrowhead was formed by constructing a great dam in 1901, which is considered by engineering authorities throughout the world to be one of the most technically perfect dams of its kind in existence. The semi-hydraulic, fill-type dam, 184 feet tall, 660 feet long, is 1,300 feet thick at the base. It has a steel-reinforced, concrete core wall in the center that is embedded 20 feet into bedrock.

Later in the 1970s, the State of California disputed these facts when it demanded major repairs of the dam, resulting in the construction of Papoose Lake.

In 1929, the Arrowhead Lake Company owned the water in Lake Arrowhead, and all the lake's water flowed naturally from the watershed from a 9.37-square-mile watershed on the upper slopes of the San Bernardino Mountains. Property owners did not own the lake.

The domestic water supply came from the lake with intake values at 110 and 140 feet below the surface of the lake, making it extremely pure for drinking. In 1928, it was stated that the community consumed about fourteen inches of surface water and that another three feet of surface water in the lake was lost to evaporation. The average rainfall over the years from 1923 to 1928 was twenty-nine and a half inches, with an average of fifty-four and a half inches of snow each of those years.

The water was piped to each lot at a minimum charge of $1.50 per meter per month. The rates for the first five hundred cubic feet per meter per month were thirty cents for one hundred cubic feet. The next five hundred cubic feet were twenty cents per one hundred cubic feet. Over one thousand cubic feet usage per month was fifteen cents per one hundred cubic feet. These rates were applied to everyone, domestic and commercial, using Lake Arrowhead's water service. Today's Lake Arrowhead water rate payers would envy these rates.

"Arrowhead Woods is the only mile-high mountain lake [elevation about 5,125 feet] in the world with a modern sewer system servicing every lot." This system would maintain the purity of the lake's water forever, the ALC claimed.

THE 1930s

The Depression affected Lake Arrowhead differently than much of California because it was not an industrial area but an isolated vacation and newly developed upscale housing area. Lake Arrowhead did not suffer many of the hardships of closed businesses since most were owned by the ALC and directed toward the upper crust. However, the area did feel some effects of the Depression. Some of the local campgrounds became safe summer refuges (and homes) away from the heat of the city for homeless families with cars, and the Dance Pavilion became a cafeteria.

Unfortunately, several of the under-financed subdivisions near Lake Arrowhead were repossessed by banks. Individuals and families who found themselves without jobs let their vacation properties go for unpaid taxes to the state or moved into them full time if it was cheaper than their larger homes.

One of the good things that occurred in 1930 was that the Southern California Edison Company purchased electrical facilities from the Arrowhead Utility Company, owned by the Arrowhead Lake Company, becoming the utility for the mountain district for $65,996, acquiring all the electrical facilities and distribution, plus the telephone system serving the Lake Arrowhead area. The Arrowhead Lake Company had been buying additional power from Edison for some time, so the Edison consolidation was a logical one and brought in some cash flow.

Between 1928 and 1933, the Rim of the World Road was straightened, improved and paved, creating a "High Gear Paved Road," making year-round access to the Lake Arrowhead area easier. This also helped the local economic recovery, as the construction created jobs. The recreational aspect of the economy of the Lake Arrowhead area had been affected because there were fewer visitors, but it also benefitted because it now had so many available hotel rooms.

Old Lake Arrowhead Village, 1930s. *Author's collection.*

There had been a lull in movie making after "talkies" were developed. But as sound recording technology improved, movie companies remembered Lake Arrowhead for its varied terrain and ability to house large numbers of people in its fine hotels, and now that the rates were discounted, Lake Arrowhead again became a movie-filming destination.

THE 1930s WERE MOVIE DAYS IN LAKE ARROWHEAD

During the 1930s and '40s, the movie industry became the basis for the economy, helping to support the Lake Arrowhead area communities during those Depression years. The movies being made at the time were full of hope and encouraged the nation to believe that better days were ahead; they also took the audiences' attention away from their current downtrodden situation. Audiences spent their nickels to escape the realities of their situations and let them enjoy their time at the theater.

Movie stars found the peaceful setting to their liking, and some built homes around the lake. They enjoyed spending time away from the Hollywood

Totem Pole Point, where five totem poles were placed and several movies were filmed. *Photo by Dick Mackey.*

crowds, experiencing the four seasons in Lake Arrowhead. The seasons of fall, with its turning leaves, and winter, with its snow, were something the East Coast actors missed and could not find elsewhere in Southern California. They had easy access to Lake Arrowhead and were still less than ninety miles from Hollywood. The area liked its movie star guests, as they added to the local economy. Not only were the cast and crew served at the hotels and restaurants, but so were set builders and production assistants. Local lumberman John Dexter installed five totem poles for the 1938 movie *Spawn of the North*, thus giving Totem Pole Point on Blue Jay Bay its name.

The mountains were used for location shots as diverse as the mountains of the Alps. For desert locations, crews shot at the Pinnacles, with forest, mountain and winter scenes representing the Canadian Rockies. Some of the films, such as *McKenna of the Mounted* (1932), *Trail of the Royal Mounted* (1932) and *The Drifter* (1932), used the Lake Arrowhead vicinity as Canada in their Royal Canadian Mounted Police movies. Lake Arrowhead Village was used frequently as a quaint European village or Paris. *Her Splendid Folly* (1933), starring Lillian Bond and Beryl Mercer, was filmed right in Lake Arrowhead Village, using the location as itself. It used the newly completed Rim of the World High Gear Road in some scenes, convincing some that it was now easier to get to the mountains. This added to the tourist business.

The Richest Girl in the World, made in 1934, has numerous lake scenes; it stars Miriam Hopkins, Joel McCrea and Fay Wray the year after she was the star in the movie *King Kong*. The story is about an extremely rich girl (Hopkins) who trades places with her secretary, played by Fay Wray. Hopkins falls for a poor but promising man (McCrea) who wants to marry her as a poor secretary, thereby proving his true love. It appealed to the desire of regular folks who wanted to know how the rich lived. It is imagined the story was inspired by the life of Barbara Hutton, who had inherited $50 million in 1933. The movie added to the allure of Lake Arrowhead as an upscale, desirable place. A nationwide search was conducted for publicity purposes for the movie *Eight Girls in a Boat*, released in 1934.

Shirley Temple, one of America's most popular Depression-era actresses, made four movies in the San Bernardino Mountains. In 1933, as a five-year-old, *To the Last Man*, based on a story written by Zane Grey, was her first full-length movie. In 1934, she starred with Carole Lombard and Gary Cooper in *Now and Forever*, shot on Lake Arrowhead's Lone Pine Island. She filmed the classic *Heidi* at Switzer Park in 1937 and, in 1940, starred in *The Blue Bird*.

Lake Arrowhead often doubled for Switzerland and did so twice in 1936. The movies *Stolen Holiday* and *Three Smart Girls* were both filmed in Lake Arrowhead by Warner Brothers. In *Three Smart Girls*, Deanna Durbin sings while sailing across Lake Arrowhead. This film also stars Ray Milland and has many beautiful scenes of sailing on the lake and at the Chateau des Fleurs, near the North Shore Tavern.

MGM built a whole Ohio riverfront village on Movie Point for the 1938 movie *Of Human Hearts*, which starred Jimmy Stewart and local homeowner Walter Huston, as well as future Lake Arrowhead resident Gene Lockhart. A paddle-wheeler steamboat was brought to the lake, causing a ruckus when a fire lookout on Butler Peak reported a fire near Lake Arrowhead. It turned out to be the steamboat belching black smoke as it sailed about the lake.

With all these actors and actresses visiting and working in the Lake Arrowhead area, and many purchasing homes or returning for vacations away from Hollywood, since they had money to spend, the movies and their stars all helped Lake Arrowhead get through the Depression years, not unscathed, but better than many places in America.

9
Winters in Lake Arrowhead

EDI JAUN, SKI EXPERT

Born in Bern, Switzerland, in 1901, Edi Jaun grew up enjoying hiking and skiing. He arrived in the San Bernardino Mountains from Pennsylvania in 1921 after Jaun's uncle heard Paul Bauman, the engineer for the Arrowhead Lake Company (ALC), was Swiss, so Edi came to California looking for a job with the ALC. He was hired to promote snow skiing and winter sports.

Because he was the only ALC employee who knew how to ski, Jaun collected the mail once a week from the mail truck on the main highway, skiing it down to the village. He also repaired downed telephone wires on skis after each snowstorm.

One of the first things Jaun accomplished was to level off a cove for an ice-skating rink, near where the village was being constructed, and he built a half-mile-long ski run from Tavern Bay toward Grass Valley and a toboggan run for the company. These were all part of the ALC's efforts at making Lake Arrowhead a four-season resort. It was not his fault that there wasn't any snow until late in the season in 1922.

Jaun purchased South Shore Marinas on the lake in 1923 and owned it and the North Shore Marinas with his nephew, Wilmer, until the 1960s. In the 1930s, he decided to adapt the art of snow skiing to the water, so there would be year-round skiing at Lake Arrowhead. Soon, Jaun's nephews—Erwin in 1934, Wilmer in 1936, Herman Wiklund in 1936 and Herman's fiancée, Helen, in 1937—moved to Lake Arrowhead. It reminded them of Switzerland. They took the water skiing idea and made it work, with Wilmer eventually owning the marinas. All became longtime residents and promoters of the community of Lake Arrowhead. They were excellent boat drivers and were used in several movies that were filmed on Lake Arrowhead, including the 1940 movie *Dulcy*, in which Wilmer did the stunt boat driving, and the 1957 movie *Mister Corey* with Tony Curtis.

In 1930, one of the best snow ski jumps in the nation was built at Big Pines, in nearby Wrightwood. Their competitions attracted professional ski jumpers from all over the world. Halvor Halstead, from Norway, came to compete, and the next year he was managing the facility. In 1934, Halstead designed a ski jump/run for Lake Arrowhead. It was located on the hill above the current Lake Arrowhead Presbyterian Church. The run went toward the village and the school (now Fire Station No. 91). Edi Jaun constructed it for the ALC.

Edi and his wife, Eli, enjoyed both cross-country skiing and jumping. Eli was one of fewer than a dozen female ski jumpers in the United States in the early 1930s. Edi and Eli both competed in the 1933 Seventh Annual Winter Sports Carnival, held at Lake Arrowhead during the massive snow year, and he won the five-mile cross-country race. She represented the Lake Arrowhead Ski Club in competitions across the state and was referred to as "Lake Arrowhead's Star Racer."

Johnny Elvrum, the 1934 long jump champion from the Big Pines competition, was hired by the Arrowhead Lake Company to promote skiing for the 1934–35 snow season featuring the new ski jump. However, there wasn't much snow that year, so Elvrum and Jaun, who was driving the school bus that winter, taught the local school kids to ski down the two-mile-long road from the highway to the school. They found they had much in common since both had European backgrounds, so they felt a kinship.

In 1938–39, Jaun and Elvrum built a 1,200-foot-long sling lift through the glen behind the schoolhouse, just outside the village. This was a safer place for the kids to ski than the roadway, and many adults have reminisced happily about using that local sling lift. It offered access to several ski runs for skill levels ranging from easy to expert. It was near both the Raven and Village Inn Hotels, making access to the sling lift easy for vacationers at Lake Arrowhead. Unfortunately, since the Lake Arrowhead area is located at only the 5,100-foot elevation level, it experienced several low snow years in a row at the resort. The ski equipment often sat idle while it rained. The ski tow was sold to Tony Crowder in the 1940s.

Jaun believed the Fish Camp fishing area near the headwaters of Deep Creek was wonderful for skiing. He and his wife and friends discovered the area and used it as their own skiing oasis, hiking up the mountainside to ski down before anything was built there. Later, he bought the concession stand there in 1938 (after borrowing $200 from Elvrum), near the rope tow that was built in 1932 by Les Salm. Jaun added ski rentals, built a warming house with a large fireplace and provided food for the skiers. Then, he, Elvrum and Salm convinced the Forest Service to rename the area Snow Valley.

The Arrowhead Springs Hotel (at the base of the mountain) purchased the Snow Valley ski business from Jaun in 1939. When Arrowhead Springs went broke in 1941, Elvrum leased the sling lifts until he was able to buy Snow Valley at auction. Lake Arrowhead promoted Elvrum's Snow Valley as its local skiing facility, and then he worked hard to create the Snow Valley Ski Resort, which continues today.

1933 WINTER CARNIVAL

The summers were great in Lake Arrowhead. In the 1930s, Lake Arrowhead Village had a great Fun Zone, with a bowling alley, miniature golf, the Dance Pavilion (with live bands) and an outdoor screen with benches for summer movies. There was even a snack bar, hamburger stand and candy shop. What more could a kid want? However, the winters were great, too.

January 1933's Mid-Winter Snow Carnival was one for the records in Lake Arrowhead—the disaster records, that is. The Mid-Winter Snow Carnival was designed to encourage visitors to drive up the newly paved and realigned Rim of the World Highway to enjoy the snow and spend some money.

The first Snow Carnival was held in Lake Arrowhead Village in 1927, attracting eight thousand snow bunnies, spectators and participants to the resort. The Snow Carnival was then held annually in different mountain locations; for example, in 1930, it was at Camp Seeley in Valley of Enchantment, drawing fifteen thousand visitors. Each year, the amount of snow on the ground for the carnival was unpredictable.

By January 26, 1933, the Snow Carnival was to be held at Lake Arrowhead Village again. The first wave of visitors excitedly began arriving just days after about fifty-five inches of the cold white stuff had fallen, more snow than had fallen for over twenty-five years. The road crews were busy trying to open the main roads in time for the carnival's opening on Saturday. The road crews stated that the roads were covered in snow and ice "but readily negotiable for cars with skid chains." Fifty-five inches of snow is quite a bit, and it's possible resort owners were concerned about the costly preparations (it was the Depression, after all) they had made for the Snow Carnival; now that there was a lot of snow, they didn't want to discourage tourists. They may not have paid much attention to the (unreliable in that day) weather forecast, predicting the possibility of more snow. The village's parking lot was mostly cleared in the anticipation of visitors.

The county and resort snowplows had succeeded in clearing one lane in each direction of the icy roadways to Lake Arrowhead Village. The turnouts were filled with snow berms from the snow removal efforts. When Saturday, the first day of the Snow Carnival, arrived, Lake Arrowhead Village's parking lot was overflowing, and hundreds more cars and busloads of visitors arrived with no place to park. Still, even more cars and trucks continued to wind their way up the snow-clogged roadways. The traffic jam was miles long and made worse because many of the Depression-era cars were attempting to come up without good tires or snow chains and sliding into the snow berms, blocking traffic.

Many of those stuck in the traffic abandoned their vehicles along the roadway and began to walk to the Snow Carnival, or those near a resort went inside to find a warm place out of the weather. Others just stayed in their vehicles, hoping the traffic snarl would clear and they'd get to the carnival soon. Every resort became filled to over capacity. The Valley View Inn, for example, which was designed for 30 guests, had over 130 jammed inside its facilities because they didn't have the heart to turn away anyone when there was nowhere else to go and no ability to drive anywhere. The situation became an emergency, since the roads were basically closed, despite the efforts of the road crews, who also couldn't get through the car-clogged roads.

The roads were so bad that some motorists were marooned, forcing them to decide whether to walk for help or stay with their cars, without a way to escape.

Then, on Sunday afternoon, another blizzard arrived with blowing snow, and those who were in their cars were blanketed with heavy snow—quite a shock for Southern Californians, many of whom knew nothing about snow.

A distress call went out to Lake Arrowhead residents, who had sleds and shovels and knew the roads, to quickly go out as search parties and rescue those stuck in their cars. The visitors needed to be brought inside to safety.

One man was found walking down the road in clothes that weren't warm enough, battling the elements and trying to go get help, as his car was stranded. His wife was found nearly frozen inside their convertible stuck in a snowdrift. A father and son were found almost dead inside their car from carbon monoxide poisoning after using their heater with their engine idling

Lake Arrowhead Village with snow. *Author's collection.*

to keep them from freezing. Even a busload of Boy Scouts had to be rescued; they were marooned in a line of stuck vehicles amongst the snowdrifts.

In addition to the weather and abandoned vehicles, a huge tree had fallen across the highway during the Sunday storm, forcing the road crews to spend hours cutting it into pieces before they could attempt to reopen the roadway. Snowplows, rotary snow blowers, hand crews and even the motorists themselves with shovels were at work trying to open the roadways. When the snow finally stopped, the Motor Transit Company sent buses with food up the mountain and transported hundreds of Snow Carnival visitors off the mountain and out of the deep snow, as food was getting scarce at the resorts and stores on the mountaintop.

However, because of the helpful nature of mountain residents and resort owners, no one died from the Mid-Winter Snow Carnival blizzard, and the injuries were actually surprisingly minor. Only one boy had badly frostbitten feet, and another fifty people were treated for frostbite. Considering the thousands stranded and rescued and the massiveness of the storms, the rescue effort could be declared a success.

SKI JUMP CHAMPION JOHN ELVRUM

The Arrowhead Lake Company tried to encourage the tourist trade in many ways. It used the tried-and-true methods that had worked in the past. It printed thousands of postcards and advertised and encouraged movies to be filmed in and around the village to promote the area to the world. But during the 1930s, the average American family was broke and didn't have any disposable income to vacation at an upscale resort.

One significant positive change the ALC effected was to hire John Elvrum to promote the winter snow season. After the winter of 1933, it was assumed the Lake Arrowhead area was quite a snow community. Elvrum changed the way Californians experienced winter in the San Bernardino Mountains for the next sixty years.

Born in Norway, John Elvrum set the U.S. amateur jump distance record of 240 feet in 1934 at Wrightwood. That day, the Arrowhead Lake Company offered Elvrum work as a ski instructor to promote skiing in the Lake Arrowhead area.

Unfortunately, the next winter of 1934–35 had very little snow, so there was not much ski promotion that season. Instead, Elvrum took it upon himself to teach the local schoolchildren and his friends to ski. He and another transplanted European, Edi Jaun, the school's bus driver, also built a small ski jump behind the school (now Fire Station No. 91). Jaun would drive the students up Two-Mile Road (now Highway 173) and have the kids ski back down to the school for recreation. They were constantly looking for better skiing areas and wanted to build a skiing rope tow up Strawberry Peak but could not get U.S. Forest Service approval.

By 1938–39, Elvrum and Jaun saw winter ski potential at the Fish Camp summer fishing resort run by the Arrowhead Springs Hotel at the headwaters of Deep Creek. It got fabulous snow and was in a natural bowl with a nearby rope tow. In 1938, Elvrum loaned Jaun $200 so he could buy the fishing concession stand there and make it a year-round operation by adding ski rentals. Then they worked to get the name changed to Snow Valley.

By 1941, the lasting effects of the Depression, followed by World War II, had slowed the growth of the entire mountain area and brought the vacation/recreation industry to a virtual standstill. The effects of gasoline rationing resulted in a significant drop in travel.

The Arrowhead Springs Hotel Corporation (at the foot of the mountain), which had bought out Jaun, went bankrupt, putting its ownership of Snow Valley on the auction block in the summer of 1941. John Elvrum, who had been working at Snow Valley, bought it for $5,000 and immediately expanded the skiing operation.

Fortunately for Elvrum, Snow Valley had several winters of snowy weather, and he encouraged skiers to stay at the nearby hotels of his former employers at Lake Arrowhead. He continued to help the ALC, as

The men responsible for bringing skiing to Lake Arrowhead, Edi Jaun (left) and John Elvrum (right). *Published with permission of* The Alpenhorn News, *courtesy Rim of the World Historical Society.*

he felt a sense of appreciation toward it for introducing him to the San Bernardino Mountains.

Elvrum operated Snow Valley, hiring local residents during the winter while they were not working at the Lake Arrowhead Village and teaching local students to ski through PE classes at the local schools through 1971, when he sold Snow Valley.

THE WAR YEARS' EFFECT

The war years were worse for Lake Arrowhead than the Depression had been. Most of the men went to fight in the war, and the women were working in war industry factories. Recreation and vacationing were not considered patriotic.

At Lake Arrowhead Village during World War II, the tourist trade virtually stopped because of gasoline rationing, so almost the only people visiting were movie companies. The ALC patriotically encouraged the village to be used as a Rest and Recuperation (R&R) location for troops, but it wasn't bringing in many dollars. Meanwhile, the bankrupt former Arrowhead Springs Hotel and Resort at the foot of the mountain became an infirmary for injured soldiers to recover. When recovered, they often came up to visit Lake Arrowhead before returning home.

The summer months were better than winter at Lake Arrowhead, as the soldiers could ride on boats, play miniature golf, watch movies and go boating and fishing. Because of gasoline rationing, not many working people used their gas stamps on long-distance drives for a vacation to the mountains. The Dance Pavilion in Lake Arrowhead Village became popular with the soldiers

A bear (foreground) sleeping in Lake Arrowhead Village. *Photo by Tony Burke; courtesy Dr. Don Adkins Collection.*

for entertainment, since many stationed at the San Bernardino Army Air Base (later, Norton Air Force Base) were living in otherwise vacant cabins in the mountains as the airbase did not have enough housing.

Lot sales at Lake Arrowhead were almost nonexistent, and many privately owned cabins sat unvisited. The world was at war, and Snow Valley was suffering financially, also. Elvrum closed the resort and joined the U.S. Army's Ski Troopers in 1943, returning in 1945. The war years had helped heavy manufacturing areas recover from the Depression but had not helped those trying to promote the resort and recreation side of the economy. The Arrowhead Lake Company was seriously suffering financially.

After almost twenty-five years of successful management of Lake Arrowhead Village and the lake, the Arrowhead Lake Company went into receivership in 1946. Its many years of financial woes had left it without the resources needed to recover. This was unfortunate because the best days for Lake Arrowhead Village were just around the corner.

10

Around Beautiful Lake Arrowhead

The North Shore Tavern/UCLA

The main building of the UCLA Conference Center, which was built in 1921 by the Arrowhead Lake Company as the North Shore Tavern, was Lake Arrowhead's most exclusive resort. At first, the only way to access the area was to be ferried across the lake from Lake Arrowhead Village.

The tavern was built at the edge of a green meadow, nestled against the hills among the pines. Nine guest cottages were built for accommodations. The main lodge building contained the dining room, lounge, large foyer and offices.

Since each vacationer had a separate cottage or lodge, it had the feeling of a private club. The North Shore Tavern often played host to famous people and movie stars, especially those who wanted seclusion away from the public's eye. Its cuisine was said to be the very best, with only the choicest of foods prepared by well-known chefs. Meals could be delivered to the cottages upon request.

The tavern also was advertised as a perfect place to bring children. "The meadow and shady spots removed from the building provide plenty of places for children to play naturally without causing annoyance to their elders," stated a 1929 brochure. It promoted its shallow bathing cove at Tavern Bay as a safe haven for children to play in the water. Today, Tavern Bay Beach Club is an exclusive retreat for Arrowhead Woods property owners.

North Shore Tavern. *Author's collection.*

The North Shore Tavern had the reputation of being a center for Roaring Twenties activities, and it has been said that they continued to roar through the 1940s. The Cedar Guest Lodge was added in the 1940s, originally to house the seasonal employees.

The tavern hosted many movie stars throughout the Depression. In 1942's *Now Voyager*, Bette Davis filmed the transformation scene on the tavern's tennis courts.

It was after World War II when the Los Angeles Turf Club purchased Lake Arrowhead. In the 1950s, the Cedar Lodge building of the North Shore Tavern became the area's grammar school. The tavern itself became the headquarters for the Lake Arrowhead Yacht Club, which was started by Thomas Hamilton of Point Hamiltair.

During its ownership years, the Turf Club divested itself of many Lake Arrowhead properties. It desired to donate the North Shore Tavern to a university, first approaching the University of Southern California (USC), but that institution declined the donation. The regents of the University of California were offered the forty-acre property, which they accepted, providing it was self-supporting and used for educational purposes.

The first conferences were held in 1958 under the supervision of UCLA. The conferences in the later 1960s came under the control of the UC Riverside Extension program. In 1982, UCLA Business Enterprises began to operate the facility, resulting in a name change to the UCLA Conference Center.

Beginning in 1984, the UCLA Conference Center was totally refurbished, maintaining the original elegant French Normandy architecture, with the addition of three new conference rooms and a new dining room. The construction of thirty-two two-story "condolets" enabled the facility to host three conferences at the same time.

Bruin Woods, the UCLA Alumni Association Family Resort Program, started in 1985, enabling families to enjoy vacations there. Twelve additional condolets were added to the property in 1990, and in 1995, thirty more were built to replace twenty-six outdated rooms.

The bark beetle infestation of the early 2000s saw many old pine trees dying on the property, and hundreds were removed, but because of the immaculate care given to the landscaping, the grounds still have that forested, alpine feeling.

The UCLA Conference Center embraces its heritage, with many large historic photographs on display throughout the facility.

HAMILTAIR POINT AND PENINSULA

Hamiltair Point and Peninsula gets its name from the Hamilton family, which owned the thirty-six acres of that large Lake Arrowhead western peninsula for almost five decades beginning in the late 1920s through the 1970s. The name "Hamiltair" was adopted from the cable address Hamilton used while working in Europe, a combination of the words "Hamilton" and "air."

Thomas Hamilton was an early day aviator and inventor who made several improvements to the design of propellers, including inventing the variable pitch propeller, which brought him fame and fortune.

Lake Arrowhead became the Hamilton family's vacation home away from Beverly Hills. In 1933, Thomas built homes there for his daughters, Ethel and Kitten. They enjoyed the connection with nature and raised produce and game, including fruits, vegetables, chickens, turkeys and milk from their five cows, selling the excess to the Lake Arrowhead Market. Several movies were filmed on the peninsula, giving it the nickname "Movie Point." It is located across Blue Jay Bay from Totem Pole Point, with five totem poles built on its tip.

Hamilton helped organize the Lake Arrowhead Yacht Club, and during the Turf Club years, the yacht club operated from the Old North Shore Tavern. Hamilton's sons, Larry and Tom Jr., bought the peninsula from the family estate when Thomas Sr. died and developed the gated Hamiltair Estates in the 1960s.

11

Santa Anita Turf Club Years

LAKE ARROWHEAD FEATURED IN PACIFIC PATHWAYS MAGAZINE

When the Santa Anita Turf Club group purchased Lake Arrowhead, it immediately set to promoting its new investment. One of the best advertising mediums in the 1940s was through magazines, and one of the first big spreads was in *Pacific Pathways* magazine.

Pacific Pathways magazine was a new thirty-five-cent, forty-five-page monthly magazine in 1946, just after World War II, with a matte finish on its thick, watercolor-paper-style pages. Articles in *Pacific Pathways* described and displayed wonderful West Coast places. The July 1946 edition spotlighted Lake Arrowhead Village. Since the Santa Anita Turf Club had just purchased Lake Arrowhead, this magazine article was part of its early advertising blitz of the beauty and glamour of the lake and village, encouraging vacationers.

With full-color pictures that stretched to the edges of the eight-and-a-half- by eleven-inch pages, it provided the illusion of panoramic views. *Pacific Pathways* was precisely aimed at the postwar driver, urging protection of the scenery by not tossing cigarettes out of car windows, thus preventing fires that would leave scars and "blight for years to come."

The sixteen-paragraph-long article extolled the beauty, fabulous amenities and proposed improvements to the recreational facilities at Lake Arrowhead with glowing adjectives, such as "waxed enthusiastic," "sumptuous" and

A full-color page from the June 1946 *Pacific Pathways* magazine of the docks and village of Lake Arrowhead after the Santa Anita Turf Club upgraded and began promoting the area. *Author's collection.*

"Land of Enchantment." The eight-page feature included seven half-page pictures, four in color; two full-page pictures, one in color; and even more black-and-white pictures.

Its purpose was to encourage vacationers to visit Lake Arrowhead, and it praised the financial investment in the property by the new owners, the Santa Anita Turf Club along with Dr. Charles Strub, who rescued the village from the receivership it suffered after the Depression years. Dr. Strub and associates, it said, had just invested $1 million to improve the classic village. Strub, the executive vice-president of the amusement center, was quoted as saying in 1946:

> *Lake Arrowhead will have a summer stock company of theater and film stars performing at the Theater of the Pines in the Village. This will be one of the greatest recreational spots in the United States...with every type of sports facility available to the public this year.*
>
> *We'll provide more horses, more boats, more ski lifts and more ski runs. The present fish hatchery is dilapidated. We'll establish one to create better facilities for trout so that the lake can become a fisherman's paradise.*

The improvements added activities and amenities, such as tennis tournaments, sail and powerboat races, water-skiing competitions, improved ice rinks, winter sleigh rides and toboggan runs, horse- and dog-pulled cart rides, a new bowling alley and skeet shooting, and would add cabanas and improve the beach next to the North Shore Tavern, which is known today as Tavern Bay Beach and Park. Since there were so many movie industry people who already owned homes in the area, the new village owners had planned to construct a radio and television broadcast facility there; however, that concept never came to fruition.

In order to lure year-round residents to the area, the village offered many full-service conveniences, including a grocery store, drugstore, gift shop, bakery and clothing stores, as well as a small hospital/doctor's office and police and fire departments.

> *Located less than 90 miles from Hollywood, and more than 5,000 feet above sea level, Lake Arrowhead with its 3,200 surrounding acres of land not only provides every type of beach and mountain sport, but also offers an exhilarating climate in the mile-high sparking air!*

Lake Arrowhead sounded like the perfect vacation wonderland, and several generations of vacationers would agree that the Turf Club did create an excellent mountain vacation resort destination.

LAKE ARROWHEAD BECOMES A VACATION DESTINATION

The Arrowhead Lake Company (ALC), which owned Lake Arrowhead and Village since the 1920s, went into receivership in 1946 because the Depression and war years, with their gasoline rationing, had created a long lull in the recreation industry. The Santa Anita Turf Club, which also owned the Santa Anita Race Track, making it flush with cash, purchased the assets of the ALC, including Lake Arrowhead, Lake Arrowhead Village and the surrounding Arrowhead Woods subdivisions and backcountry for $2 million.

The Turf Club had gambling dollars to invest, and within the first several years, it spent millions of dollars on upgrades to the somewhat run-down and neglected Lake Arrowhead Village. Investing in a different area of recreation had significant tax advantages for the Turf Club.

During the Turf Club's ownership, income generated by lot sales was not very important to it, as it had been for the Arrowhead Lake Company, so the promotion of property sales was put on the back burner; very few lots were sold, and no new residential areas were developed. But it did encourage the movie companies to continue to come and film, staying in the hotels, spending their money and providing a steady supply of movie stars for the regular visitors to admire.

However, a mini population boom began occurring in the surrounding communities in those early postwar boom years. Larger grocery stores and the numbers of students in schools reflected the growing year-round residential population. Jensen's Market opened in Blue Jay in the later 1940s and then moved to the building now occupied by Coldwell Banker Real Estate.

The Turf Club very generously donated some of its undeveloped lands over the years to worthy organizations. Its donations changed the direction and appearance of the Lake Arrowhead area and how it developed.

The Turf Club donated land for a new elementary school, as the student population had outgrown the four-room school built in the 1920s. Then the old school site was donated to the volunteer Lake Arrowhead Fire Department, which is still in use by the Lake Arrowhead County Fire Department as Station No. 91, located just outside the entrance of Lake Arrowhead Village on Highway 189.

The Boy and Girl Scouts each received campgrounds from the Turf Club, while the State of California was given the original North Shore Tavern to use as a conference center for the state university system, now run by the

The 1946 set for the movie *The Yearling* at Lake Arrowhead. *Author's collection, donated by Lee Cozad.*

University of California at Los Angeles (UCLA). It also donated land to the county and to local churches.

The nuns of the Sisters of St. Joseph of Orange were given land and an additional $50,000 to build a community hospital for the Sisters to operate. The newly constructed hospital was featured in the 1956 movie *Magnificent Obsession*, with Rock Hudson and Jayne Wyman. That same hospital is now Mountains Community Hospital.

The Turf Club had money to spend, and it spent it promoting the advantages of visiting the Lake Arrowhead area during summer or winter. Smaller surrounding resorts and activities piggybacked on the massive advertising budget of Lake Arrowhead Village. Fortunately, the weather cooperated and encouraged Southern Californians' desire to visit. The summers were wonderful; the village hired local people, and many small business owners were able to develop popular businesses such as the family-owned McKenzie Water Ski School, which is still in operation in 2015.

Vacationers could get "back to nature" by camping, hiking, horseback riding, fishing, water skiing and boating in the Lake Arrowhead area. The trees of the forest, the lake, the clear skies and the many amenities the village offered appealed to the typical postwar family.

Snow Valley Ski Resort. *Author's collection.*

The winter of 1948–49 arrived early with lots of snow, and the public lined up to try out the new snow lifts at Snow Valley. Former Arrowhead Lake Company employee John Elvrum had purchased Snow Valley prior to the war. With Elvrum reopening the Snow Valley Ski slopes, the village and local hotels began promoting their proximity to it, reinforcing the idea that Lake Arrowhead was a true year-round tourist destination. Elvrum built the first steel tower ski lift in Southern California at Snow Valley. He personally maintained and operated the ten rope tows and the double chair lifts. He was a hands-on owner and operated the lifts for over twenty years. He employed many Lake Arrowhead residents every winter, and many of those same families worked the summer jobs in Lake Arrowhead Village. These happy, friendly local residents added to the image and allure of Lake Arrowhead as a four-season resort. Snow Valley was the most popular ski resort in the San Bernardino Mountains in the 1950s. Elvrum advertised his resort seasonally and printed thousands of postcards. The 1950s began the glory years for Lake Arrowhead Village. Magazines and newspapers, both nationwide and locally, loudly touted the beauty, activities, facilities and fun of the area.

The thousands of picture-postcards sold annually were more than just tools for sending greetings home; they were another "free" form of publicity. The cool breezes through the pine trees, the sailboats, water skiing, shopping at the village, the arcades for the kids, ice skating at Blue Jay, movies, Lake Arrowhead's sandy beach and the nine-hole golf course offered all the attractions 1950s tourists wanted. They could experience luxury at the high-

Santa Anita Hospital (now Mountains Community Hospital). The land and money to build it were donated by the Turf Club to improve the amenities of the mountain community. *Author's collection.*

quality resort hotels and enjoy the village and the lake activities. Movie star sightings were a real possibility, too.

Many movie and television stars had second homes at Lake Arrowhead. Hollywood stars continued to have vacation homes in this beautiful pine forest location, where they felt thousands of miles away from the hustle and bustle of Hollywood and yet could drive to the city in just a couple of hours.

Six weeks before the opening of Disneyland in Anaheim, the Henck family created a corporation and built the family amusement park of Santa's Village, opening in their meadow in Skyforest, just three miles from Lake Arrowhead. Santa's Village advertised on television, brought up TV personalities and promoted many special events each year—additional reasons to vacation in the Lake Arrowhead area year round. The Lake Arrowhead area became well known, not only in California, but also nationwide, and it increased in popularity.

LAKE ARROWHEAD BECOMES SOUTHERN CALIFORNIA'S VACATION DREAM

The Rim of the World Unified School District was formed in 1954, uniting the Running Springs, Crest Forest and Lake Arrowhead Elementary School Districts, which had been formed in the later 1920s. A high school was built in its current location on the Rim of the World Highway, which was adjacent to K-8 Lake Arrowhead Elementary School at the time. Rim of the World High School had its first graduating class, with forty-one students, in 1957.

The 1950s were the glory years for the village. Many Southern California families visited Lake Arrowhead Village annually, bringing their out-of-state guests. The cool summer breezes through the pine trees, the sailboats, the arcade with its swinging cages and even a small steam locomotive traveling out to the point offered all the attractions the 1950s tourist could imagine.

The idea of driving to Lake Arrowhead became more palatable when the state, in 1956, announced it would create four-lane freeway access all the way to Big Bear by realigning the windy, two-lane, 1930s Rim of the World mountain road. The first and only section of that freeway, from San Bernardino to the Crestline Bridge, was completed in the mid-1960s. The lack of a four-lane highway to the mountains did delay intensified residential building, but the recreation industry continued to thrive.

Many movie and television stars purchased second homes at Lake Arrowhead. Some of the better-known show business families were television and movie stars like the Ozzie Nelson family, the Lockharts and the Von Zells. Even future stars such as the Wilson family, of the 1960s surf music band the Beach Boys, had vacation homes in the area. In 1956, Blue Jay Village hosted a parade with Shirley Temple as the grand marshal, honoring her for the four movies she had made in the mountain community.

Lake Arrowhead's proximity to Hollywood, the new highway and the atmosphere of closeness to nature in an upscale setting attracted the stars and lured many more to this mountain paradise.

The Turf Club owned Lake Arrowhead Village until 1960, when the tax laws changed and it could no longer deduct losses from one business (Lake Arrowhead Village) from its profits on another unrelated business (Santa Anita Race Track).

The Turf Club sold Lake Arrowhead, but the desirable community image had already been created.

A SWINGIN' SUMMER FILMED AT LAKE ARROWHEAD

Advertized with the catchy "Spread out the beach towels, grab your gals, it's gonna be *A Swingin' Summer*," the Hollywood musical comedy movie escapade

A poster for movie *A Swingin' Summer*, filmed in Lake Arrowhead in 1964. *Author's collection.*

features a group of three friends who choose to spend their "beach vacation" not in the crashing waves of the ocean but rather at Lake Arrowhead, with its abundant water sports, working at promoting concerts at the Dance Pavilion in the village when they discover it is in danger of closing.

William Wellman Jr. (Rick) and James Stacy (Mickey) run into conflict when the local lifeguard, Martin Wesrt (Turk), tries to ruin their plans by hiring goons and stealing Rick's girlfriend. At the same time, Quinn O'Hara (Cindy) arranges for her rich dad to finance the financially strapped Dance Pavilion. The bookworm, Raquel Welch (Jeri) in her first movie, lets down her hair, singing and dancing, and problems ensue.

Many scenes feature Old Lake Arrowhead Village, with action scenes on the lake and lots of cute bikini-clad teenage girls. The movie previews of the era announced, "They're Lovin', Laughin', and Livin' it up and for kicks playing Chicken on Water Skis."

The eighty-minute Technicolor *A Swingin' Summer* was filmed entirely in Lake Arrowhead during the summer of 1964 and released during the summer of 1965. The movie's assistant producer and technical advisor, Larry Mole Parker, was nineteen years old that summer, working as the manager of the Lake Arrowhead Pavilion, when his personal story became a subplot in the film. The movie showcased rock stars of the era, including Gary Lewis and the Playboys, the Righteous Brothers, the Rip Cords and Donnie Brooks as part of the plot. In the typical teen movie style of the 1960s, the fun-loving teens enjoy goofing off, water-skiing and causing trouble at the lake, all with a backdrop of music. That summer, more teens came to visit the Lake Arrowhead area as the movie made the resort a cool place to visit.

LAKE ARROWHEAD DEVELOPMENT COMPANY HEADS IN A NEW DIRECTION

In 1960, Jules Berman purchased Lake Arrowhead, the village and the 3,200 acres surrounding it for $6.5 million. Berman had made his fortune importing Kahlua from Mexico and was interested in the undeveloped lands of Arrowhead Woods so he could build high-quality residential areas through his Lake Arrowhead Development Company.

He commissioned the drafting of a master plan for the area, intending to sell lots. To attract the upscale buyers, he had the former "cow pasture" nine-hole golf course that had fallen into disrepair totally redesigned into

The new Lake Arrowhead Country Club clubhouse. *Author's collection.*

a tournament-level, high-quality, eighteen-hole golf course. Golf course designer Billy Bell, who also designed the Palm Springs Canyon Country Club golf course in 1963, laid out the design, which involved carving the back nine holes out of the mountainside. This is when the double A-frame clubhouse was designed and built and the Lake Arrowhead Country Club was established.

Attending the grand opening of the clubhouse were Bob Hope, Dean Martin, Bing Crosby and Tony Bennett. Bob Hope, Frankie Avalon and Conrad Hilton were known to play frequently on the new golf course. In September 1978, the members of the country club purchased the clubhouse and tennis courts from California Golf and turned it into a member-owned private-equity country club. Berman refurbished Lake Arrowhead Village. During the Berman years, many homes were constructed, and the population rose as the number of vacation homeowners skyrocketed.

Berman merged his Lake Arrowhead Development Company with Boise Cascade Corporation in 1967. During their ownership of the lake, the 1971 Sylmar earthquake struck, which got the attention of the

The first tee of the Lake Arrowhead Country Club golf course. The 1995 movie *Space Jam* starring Michael Jordan and Warner Bros. cartoon characters was filmed on the seventh green of this golf course. *Author's collection.*

California Department of Safety of Dams, leading to problems for the aging dam.

As the years progressed, movie stars continued to move to and vacation in the Lake Arrowhead area. Liberace, Doris Day and Andy Devine all bought homes at Lake Arrowhead. Their presence added luster to the image of the area. The communities, in return, honored the stars yet respected their privacy. This tolerant and respectful atmosphere was what lured some of the current residents to the mountain.

The Lake Arrowhead area and surrounding communities now have a year-round population of around fifty thousand, with hundreds of thousands of visitors each year. It is said the San Bernardino National Forest is the most densely populated and most visited National Forest west of the Mississippi and, possibly, nationwide.

THE LAKE CONTROVERSY

Although Papoose Lake wasn't built until the 1970s, its origins can be traced directly back to the construction of Lake Arrowhead Dam, which began eighty years before, in the 1890s.

Lake Arrowhead was built in stages and had construction difficulties, including a leaking core wall that took several engineers and years to repair. According to Gordon W. Dukleth from the Department of Safety of Dams, the Lake Arrowhead Dam was finally completed in 1922 after over thirty years of construction.

During the Sylmar earthquake, the complete failure of the Van Norman Dam endangered millions of lives. "After the Sylmar earthquake in 1971, all twenty-nine privately owned hydraulic-filled dams in the state were ordered inspected, and only two were found to be safe," said Dukleth.

During the summer of 1973, the Lake Arrowhead Dam underwent extensive testing. The 675-foot-long, 150-foot-tall Lake Arrowhead Dam was declared by Pioneer Consultants of Redlands to be unsafe in an earthquake of 6.5 or greater on the Richter scale. The dam and lake sit close to two faults, the San Andreas, eight miles to the west, and the San Jacinto, only thirteen miles away. However, without an earthquake, the dam was determined to be safe.

In August, the downstream property owners were notified of the dangers to them and to the users of the forest as far downstream as the Mojave Forks Dam. The report said boaters and swimmers in Lake Arrowhead would also be endangered if the dam collapsed. Property above the lake's water line wouldn't suffer damage from the dam's collapse.

The DSOD concluded that to guarantee the safety of the dam and those downstream, remedial dam strengthening work must occur. The repair would take time, both in design and execution. Their plan required that the lake must be lowered seventy feet below its current water level to reduce the hazard. After the repair was engineered, the repair work could begin. This sequence would take years.

The reason for the drastic action by the DSOD was that with the lake full, failure of the dam during an earthquake would cause a wall of water to rush down Little Bear and Deep Creeks to the Mojave River at speeds in excess of twenty-five miles per hour. The loss of life and property damage, said the DSOD, would be related to the height and speed of the wall of water. There are twenty-nine dwellings in the path of the inundation two miles below the dam. Three of the dwellings are permanent residences; the other twenty-six were occupied during the summer months. It was also estimated that more than two hundred persons use the canyons on summer weekends. The lake's owner, Boise Cascade Corporation, decided to drain the lake by seventy feet rather than spend the money to reinforce the dam.

The Lake Arrowhead Property Owners Association sent out "a call to action" in October 1973 to write letters informing public officials of the ramifications of the DSOD report. Then it filed a "class action lawsuit that inhibited the lake owners [either the Chicago Group or Boise Cascade] from taking unilateral action with little concern for the property owners' interest and welfare."

During a December 11, 1973 Department of Water Resources meeting at the San Bernardino Convention Center, Samuel B. Nelson told the three to four hundred audience members that it was necessary to drain the lake by seventy feet to permit reinforcement of the dam:

When the big earthquake hits, a hydraulic-filled dam turns to liquid. Lake Arrowhead holds about 48,000 acre-feet of water (making it about two-thirds the size of Silverwood Lake, which was constructed in 1971). If the dam turned to liquid, that wall of water would take everything before it. Even if there were no loss of life, should the dam break, property values would be destroyed, for it would take a long time to rebuild the dam and even longer for rainfall to refill the lake.

Of course, property owners decried that scenario and proclaimed the dam higher, thicker and stronger than the consultants said. The timing was especially bad financially because Boise Cascade was foreclosing on the Chicago Group that had purchased the lake three years before from Boise Cascade.

Controversy immediately arose regarding who was going to pay for the estimated $5 million in repairs. Would it be the three thousand small property owners of homes around the lake or Boise Cascade (or the Chicago Group), which owned the lake and dam, or would it be the thirty-five endangered homeowners downstream from the dam on Little Bear and Deep Creeks?

Community members became outraged and concerned over the uncertainty and possible loss of property values. A public meeting at Rim High School gave residents a chance to voice their concerns and to acquire facts.

Residents questioned the threat to health and safety in relation to the domestic water supply if the lake was lowered, the supply of water for fire protection and the ecological effect on fish and the watershed compared to the minimal risk to life and property created by the dam and its impounded waters. Behind their statements, they knew Lake Arrowhead property values would plummet and the aesthetic beauty of the area would be shattered by dropping the lake seventy feet and that their expensive boats would be sitting in dust. They didn't trust Boise Cascade, and residents feared they would be stuck with an unusable lake.

The DSOD stated on March 1, 1974, that an order would be given to lower the lake level unless remedial action was swiftly taken. Another delay occurred as the Department of Water Resources ordered an Environmental Impact Report, which stated that dropping the water level would have significant financial impact on the region's real estate and economy.

The private ownership of the lake was both a stumbling block and a motivator for residents. There was a real fear among some homeowners that if government money was accepted, the lake might become public. Boise Cascade stated that it was unwilling to pay the entire repair cost or subsidize a new dam, contending that it was a "community problem." But the various property owner associations were unwilling to pay for a new dam when they had no ownership of the lake.

There were several ideas proposed on how to resolve the problem. Engineer Ralph Wagner recommended fixing the old dam by adding additional support to the downstream side of the dam. This repair idea would not require the draining of the lake. That repair, however, would cost at least $2 million; Boise Cascade again refused to pay.

The Lake Arrowhead Property Owners Association, led by Hal Pierce, Ed Duarte and Bob Everhart, began negotiating with Boise Cascade and concluded that the best solution would likely be the construction of a new downstream dam, an idea that Boise Cascade accepted but wouldn't fund (with its $5 million price tag). However, the company saw a recreational advantage with additional land being created in that proposal. Both sides sought legal opinions on the technicalities required to keep the lake private and/or owned by the residents.

In March 1974, the San Bernardino County Board of Supervisors approved assemblyman Jerry Lewis's legislation (SB 2141) to authorize the formation of an improvement zone around the lake, which could issue bonds to construct a new dam. The bonds could be repaid by property taxes generated from within the improvement zone. Lewis introduced the bill on April 22.

On June 6, the DSOD restated that satisfactory progress was not occurring on the dam's safety issues, so the water level of Lake Arrowhead would be lowered, effective September 1, 1974. At least property owners could enjoy that last summer with a full lake. The water would be released at a rate of two feet a month until it reached the level of seventy feet below the spillway. It would be a long process.

However, the next day, June 7, an agreement was signed by the Lake Arrowhead Property Owners Association, Hamiltair Property Owners Association and Boise Cascade to provide for the transfer of ownership of the lake, the dam and other real property to a corporation composed of the property owners. But that would occur only if all aspects of the lake proposal, including funding and building, went in Boise Cascade's chosen direction.

After months of negotiations among the interested parties, a meeting was held at Mary Putnam Henck Intermediate School on June 8, 1974, with of all the various property owner associations, Lake Arrowhead, Hamiltair, Meadow Bay and other interested groups, including Friends of Lake Arrowhead, the Lake Arrowhead Chamber of Commerce, local realtors and officials from San Bernardino County and Boise Cascade, in attendance. Arrowhead Woods Property Owners wanted to ensure that Lake Arrowhead remained private with enough beautiful water to retain property values.

The announced goal was to "protect Lake Arrowhead for the integrity of both its uniqueness and its property value." A hearing was scheduled at the San Bernardino County Board of Supervisors' meeting on June 11 to discuss "the consideration of the formation of an Improvement Zone in County Area #70 for the purpose of repair of the dam." The service area was approved and empowered to finance the construction of a new dam downstream from the older dam and conduct an election for the bond indebtedness.

The supervisors, seven days later, discussed and approved the formation of a County Service Area to construct a new dam. On June 18, 1974, legislative counsel George Murphy issued an opinion that a new dam constructed with taxes from the bond issued "would create no new rights of public access or use in Lake Arrowhead, as long as the water in the new lake was not commingled with Lake Arrowhead's water."

On July 5, 1974, Senate Bill 2141, hand-carried for expediency through the legislature by assemblyman Jerry Lewis (it was passed in just three days), was signed by the governor to place a bond issue on the November ballot.

THE $EVEN-MILLION-DOLLAR QUESTION

Measure G would incur an indebtedness of $7 million for Improvement Zone D-1 of County Service Area #70 for flood protection. Measure H set the tax rate for the same zone not to exceed ten cents per $100 of assessed real property value to be used for the maintenance of the flood protection facilities. Both would require a two-thirds majority to pass.

Then, on August 16, the Board of Supervisors designated Improvement Zone D-1 within Service Area 70 with a bonded indebtedness of $7 million and determined the boundaries for the district. It included all the areas of Arrowhead Woods with lake rights, excluding the Lakewood Tracks A and B, which are located near Kuffel Canyon Road.

The Department of Water Resources decided on August 23 that, since the issue was on the November ballot, it would postpone lowering the lake's level until after the election in November. It just hoped a major earthquake wouldn't occur before the election. The Arrowhead community, however, was not united behind this new dam plan, and there was strong vocal opposition. Full-blown election campaigning began. The challenge was to fully inform everyone of the measure so all would fully understand the plan, its implications and the "dire results" if the measure did not pass in the November election.

Non-full-time resident property owners were requested to change their voting registrations so they would be able to have a voice and vote on this measure.

What would occur if the $7 million bond issue failed? These were the talking points given by the "Give a Dam" supporters in September 1974:

1. The depth of the water at the dam would be lowered by 70 feet, from a height of 5,106.7 above sea level to the 5,037-foot elevation.

2. The capacity of the lake would decrease to 14,000 acre feet from 48,000 acre feet—a loss of 38,000 acre feet.

3. The lake's surface area would decrease from 780 acres to 370 acres.

4. The 410 acres of exposed lake bottom would be covered in sediments, rendering them unusable.

5. Those exposed sediments would rot, decay and probably stink.

6. When it rained, those exposed sediments would be washed back into the lake unless quickly (and expensively) removed. When washed into the lake, the depth in the lake would decrease, causing algae growth and odor, destroying the taste of the water.

7. The shoreline would be decreased from 12.5 miles to 5.3 miles.

8. All 1,500 boat docks and slips would be sitting in the dirt after the lake level dropped the first 15 feet.

9. All three sand beaches would be far from the water.

10. The domestic water system from Lake Arrowhead would become unusable because the water intake pipes would be above water level.

11. Lake Arrowhead would need a new source of water for domestic use since it was not connected to the state water project or the Crestline Lake Arrowhead Water Agency (CLAWA), which would cause water rates to increase dramatically.

12. Since most fishing occurred from docks or the shore and the boats would be sitting in the mud, most fishing would cease.

13. Tourism would immediately drop by 50 percent in Cedar Glen and Arrowhead Woods, with an expected 40 percent drop in Blue Jay. This would result in a 37 percent decline in employment and drop in tax revenue. Unless the situation changed, there wasn't much hope of economic revival.

14. Property values would drop in Arrowhead Woods by as much as 50 percent for lakefront homes, with a total loss expected to exceed $77 million.

15. The decline in property values would extend to a decrease in assessed valuation of property, leading to a decrease in tax revenues, costing the area over $2.15 million lost to its schools, fire department, sanitation district and hospital district and over $600,000 directly to the county.

16. Most native trees and plants around the lake would die.

Is it any wonder why "Give a Dam" was on everyone's lips during the summer and fall of 1974 leading up to the November election? Still, there was vocal opposition to the expense and complications of purchasing the private lake and building a new dam.

The Arrowhead Woods election on November 5, 1974, was decisive on both ballot measures. The vote was 90 percent in favor of Measures G and H.

The community voted loud and clear that it did not want the lake lowered seventy feet. The new dam needed to be started by April 1, 1975, and completed by September 1, 1976. If the deadlines were not met, the DSOD could still order the level of Lake Arrowhead lowered.

The property owners agreed with Boise Cascade that they (as a community corporation) would purchase the lake and other properties for a sum of $500,000. Boise Cascade had already been ordered to divest itself of the lake (after its conflict with the Chicago Group), so the timing for it was excellent. Boise Cascade deeded the land necessary for the new dam to San Bernardino County and advanced the funds necessary to prepare the plans for the new dam.

THE ARROWHEAD LAKE ASSOCIATION IS CREATED AND THE NEW DAM IS BUILT

The Arrowhead Lake Association (ALA) of property owners was organized pursuant to the June 1974 agreement with the various homeowners associations to pass the bond issue, build the dam and have a legal corporation to purchase the lake. The members of the interim board were: President Robert Everhart, G. Thomas Akin, Richard Anderson, Donald Coughlin, Charles Luciano, Eugene Newcombe, Karl Rodi, Ralph Wagner and Anthony Zehenni.

The contract to build the dam went out to bid, but none of the bids was low enough. The contract was modified to eliminate the landscaping and other items not directly tied to the construction of the dam. Hubbs Construction was awarded the contract on April 28, 1975 (only twenty-five days tardy), and work began in May. By August of that year, the construction of the dam was underway, with an optimistic completion date of October 1976, only one month after the Measure G deadline date. Fill materials for the earthen dam were taken from county land and Boise Cascade property east of the hospital.

The negotiations to purchase the lake for $500,000 were not as smooth sailing. The ALA needed to finance the initial $150,000 down payment to buy Lake Arrowhead, Grass Valley Lake, the old dam, the three beach club sites, all of the reserve strips and reserve strip additions and other properties within Arrowhead Woods. It figured out a five-year repayment schedule from lake revenues. The remaining $350,000 would be paid to Boise Cascade over the next ten years, also from lake revenues.

By August 1975, the ALA wanted to cash out of the deal but was unable to get the additional funds. One plan to raise the funds, the ALA decided, was to charge all holders of dock site rights a one-time fee that would enable them to have legal title to their sites. Then the dock title could be sold as real property, and the ALA would reduce dock fees in exchange.

Also, in August, the ALA was looking for elected board members. To become an ALA member and vote for the new twelve-member ALA Board of Directors, property owners had only to return a postcard by August 14, although no membership fee amount had yet been determined. All members were qualified to run for the board. The community's property owners created the Arrowhead Lake Association (ALA) to purchase and then manage their lake. The community had accepted an expensive burden to maintain the water in its beautiful private lake.

The new ALA board was elected and took office in September 1975. However, dam construction hit some snags. Change orders raised the price; delays were constant because of frozen ground, rain, snow and other weather problems; and bedrock was deeper underground than estimated—the very same problems that had plagued the construction of the original Lake Arrowhead Dam in the early 1900s.

In November 1975, the San Bernardino County Board of Supervisors appointed eight members to the newly established CSA 70-D-1 Commission to oversee the dam's construction and maintenance. There were several plan modifications during the dam construction, mostly to keep the project under budget.

The CSA-70 D-1 discovered that the interest on the bonds was being deposited in the county's general fund and realized that with those interest funds, a landscaping/anti-erosion plan could be developed and implemented. It met with county supervisor Nancy Smith and got the county policy changed, using those funds to hire forester Jim Asher, who created a three-phase plan. The interest flowed into the project fund beginning in July 1976.

September 1976's Tropical Storm Kathleen's rains rushed down the steep slopes of the project, creating deep ruts from runoff, especially above Torrey Pines Road. The Lahonton Regional Water Quality Control Board became alarmed and issued a cease-and-desist order to stop the flow of silt into Little Bear Creek. Remedial action was immediately undertaken.

In December 1976, rainwater and water siphoned through a twelve-inch pipe from Lake Arrowhead began filling the lake area behind the new dam only three months after the deadline date set by the DSOD.

It was obvious to all that the dam was not finished, but in April 1977, Hubb Construction filed for completion of the contract, asking for final payment, despite complaints from the ALA, CSA-70 D-1 and Metropolitan Advertising Agency (which had bought out Boise Cascade). The objectors contended that all the work in the contract had not been done, and both sides sued. The county settled the suits, and additional work was done by another contractor and billed to CSA-70 D-1.

But this legal stuff didn't hinder the community. The Soroptimists, Boy Scouts, Baptist Church, Rim High and Elementary students and other community groups planted the six thousand trees purchased by the Rotary Club and other groups to complete Asher's landscaping plans and stop the erosion.

The "El Nino" winter of 1977–78 saw over eighty inches of rainfall in Lake Arrowhead, forcing water to flow over Lake Arrowhead Dam's spillway and causing additional flood damage.

The new lake was filled but holds only two thousand acre-feet of water. The county applied for federal disaster funds, receiving $53,000 to cover $400,000 in damage and resulting in a service charge of $27 being assessed to all Arrowhead Woods property owners.

PAPOOSE LAKE

Lake Arrowhead's chamber of commerce, under President Dick Pretzinger, held a "Name the Lake Contest" with a $100 prize. It was the first time in San Bernardino County history that a lake was named in a contest. Lural Schafer chose the winning name of Papoose Lake. Schafer, who was a member of the exclusive Club San Moritz in Crestline, wrote for the club's monthly magazine, the *Yodeler*, and was a founding member of the Crest Forest Historical Society. Lural told me she chose the name because the $7.7 million expense of the dam was on the backs of Lake Arrowhead property owners, and with its immediate proximity to Lake Arrowhead, it was "like a papoose cradle on the back of a squaw."

Christening ceremonies were held on June 2, 1979. At the dedication ceremony, Lural poured champagne onto the rock bearing the bronze plaque naming the body of water "Papoose Lake." The plaque was stolen within weeks; the chamber replaced it and attached it to an even larger boulder. However, the new plaque has, again, "gone missing."

Since 1980, liability issues have arisen, so the thirty-two-acre, 160-foot-deep Papoose Lake is currently closed to recreational use, is self-insured and has a fence surrounding it. In accordance with all agreements between the U.S. Forest Service and the State Fish and Game Commission, Papoose Lake must discharge approximately 100 to 193 gallons of water per minute into Little Bear Creek, and the water in Papoose Lake cannot be used for recreation, only for fire protection purposes. The dam's indebtedness bonds

Above: Papoose Lake supports the downstream side of Lake Arrowhead Dam, seen on the right with the road going over it. Beyond is Lake Arrowhead. *Author's collection.*

Left: Statue dedicated to Detective Jeremiah MacKay in Lake Arrowhead Village. *Photo by Rhea-Frances Tetley.*

were paid off in 1990. The county now maintains the site as a resource conservation zone to protect the downstream landowners.

One of the major supporters of the Papoose Lake and dam project from its inception through its completion was Audrey MacKay, who was an original CSA-70 D-1 commissioner and was a longtime Lake Arrowhead manager's executive secretary under several lake managers. The dam was subsequently named the Audrey MacKay Dam in her honor.

In 2013, a long-delayed park was finally created on the bluff that overlooks Papoose Lake. The Audrey MacKay Park's name was quickly changed to MacKay Park to also honor her grandson, Detective Jeremiah MacKay, who was gunned down in the line of duty. A bronze statue of hometown hero Jeremiah MacKay on a marble base was unveiled in Lake Arrowhead Village in 2013, honoring his actions trying to find cop-killer Christopher Dorner, who was hiding out, terrorizing the Big Bear area. MacKay was ambushed as he arrived at the scene, just before the cabin Dorner was holed up in burned to the ground during live, nationwide TV coverage, with the cop killer inside. The community was shocked that Jeremiah, a three-generation Lake Arrowhead family member, died this way.

THE NEW VILLAGE

The Arrowhead Development Company merged with Boise Cascade. It sold the lake and beaches to Arrowhead Woods residents in 1975, with the construction of Papoose Dam and Lake. The lodge and village were sold to the Metropolitan Advertising Agency, which then sold it to George Coult and his GC Properties.

GC Properties wanted a new commercial village and hotel complex because the electrical wiring was old, the water pipes corroding and the old 1920s buildings showing their age. Despite strong community protest, the businesses were forced to move out of the village.

In 1979, a "Burn to Learn" exercise allowed various local fire agencies to purchase a building for one dollar to analyze how it would burn; they would set it on fire, fight the fire and again analyze if they were correct—the science part of fire science. All buildings in the village, except the steepled round dance/casino building and outer buildings, the post office, bank and a real estate office, were burned to the ground.

Old Lake Arrowhead Village, 1960s. *Author's collection.*

"Burn to Learn"—the Rialto Fire Department burning the old village.
Photo by Chuck McCleur, author's collection.

Building the new village around the old circular casino building. *Author's collection.*

The new two-story village was constructed with an alpine theme and contains shops for both residents and visitors on two different levels and parking areas on the property. The 1982 grand opening of the 176-room Hilton Arrowhead Lodge hotel was a star-studded affair with former president Gerald Ford, comedian Bob Hope and actress Phyllis Diller in attendance at the ribbon-cutting and banquets. After the new Lake Arrowhead Village was completed, the values of the homes and other property around the lake skyrocketed, and some say Lake Arrowhead is now the "Gem of the San Bernardino Mountains."

12

The Twenty-First Century

THE 2003 OLD FIRE ATTACKS CEDAR GLEN

Dick Pretzinger has worn many hats in the Lake Arrowhead Community. In the first decade of the twenty-first century, he was known for heading the Cedar Glen Redevelopment Commission after the devastating 2003 Old Fire that destroyed the Hook Creek residential area of Cedar Glen. Leading his community was not a new position for Pretzinger.

Pretzinger first visited Lake Arrowhead during his honeymoon in 1946, vacationing in Crest Park frequently throughout the 1950s and then choosing to move to the mountains in 1963. He was a surveyor, running his business from his Hook Creek home. He knew the uniqueness of the community like few others.

Just two years after Pretzinger had moved to the mountain, in 1965, the financially strapped Santa Anita Hospital was about to be closed by the Sisters of St. Joseph of Orange. Pretzinger convinced others to join with him in forming a nonprofit corporation to purchase the hospital and land and drew the boundaries for the Lake Arrowhead Hospital District, which voters approved in 1967. This hospital now serves the residents as Mountains Community Hospital. Each summer, the hospital auxiliary raises funds through its Le Grand Picnic in the hospital's beautiful rose garden on the bluffs overlooking the lake.

As a past president of the Lake Arrowhead Chamber of Commerce (1969, 1979), Pretzinger was involved in the naming and dedication ceremony of Papoose Lake, helping Lural Schafer pour the champagne over the dedication plaque. He was appointed by the county supervisor as a member of the Lake Arrowhead Municipal Advisory Council, serving for several years, and he headed several unsuccessful attempts to incorporate Lake Arrowhead into a city.

The 2003 Old Fire that began on October 25 and lasted until November 4, 2003, burned 940 homes and ninety-one thousand acres and cost $37 million to fight. Six people died, most due to the stress from being forced to evacuate. Lake Arrowhead residents were evacuated from the mountain for two weeks due to the intentional act of an arsonist who is now sitting on death row. The fire jumped Highway 18 east of Santa's Village, attacking Cedar Glen. In the Hook Creek area of Cedar Glen, 300 homes were destroyed. A snowstorm ended the advance of flames.

The County Board of Supervisors established the Cedar Glen Redevelopment Commission after the Old Fire. Pretzinger was appointed to the commission for his expertise and knowledge as a surveyor and for understanding the issues faced by burn victims because his own home was one of those destroyed by the Old Fire. Pretzinger utilized his deep knowledge of the community, and he educated the county officials as they struggled with plans to rehabilitate the area, including zoning, roads and the ancient water system. He fought the good fight for the burned-out residents of the community, not for the politicians, until his death.

In 2015, parts of Cedar Glen will still face serious rebuilding difficulties more than ten years after the fire. Now, rebuilding has stalled because the state defunded redevelopment districts before the infrastructure of Cedar Glen was restored, forcing many burned-out victims—because of the subsequent economic downswing—to abandon their land for the taxes owed.

THE 2007 GRASS VALLEY FIRE

The 2007 Grass Valley Fire began when electrical lines fell during a high-wind episode on October 22, 2007, the very same day a fire broke out' in the community of Green Valley Lake, northwest of Running Springs. Having two fires to fight taxed the firemen, but soon reinforcements

Enjoying living the good life at Lake Arrowhead. *Photo by Rhea-Frances Tetley.*

arrived; residents were evacuated, and the mountain was closed to automobile traffic.

The fire started near Deer Lodge Park and quickly spread southward, destroying and damaging 199 homes in the vicinity of the Lake Arrowhead Country Club in Grass Valley. Fortunately, most residents and weekend homeowners had significant insurance, since the homes were each valued in the $500,000 to $1 million price range, but the losses in memories were significant. Many had no more time than to evacuate their residences with little more than the clothes on their backs. The golf course assisted in creating a clearance and halted the advancement of flames in that direction.

LAKE ARROWHEAD TODAY

Lake Arrowhead, with the rebuilt village after the intentional burning in 1979, today remains a quaint mountain resort, with 12,424 full-time

The movie *The American President* used the UCLA Conference Center (former North Shore Tavern) as a stand-in for Camp David in 1995. *Author's collection, courtesy Lee Cozad.*

residents (according to the 2010 census). Lake Arrowhead attracts nearly 100,000 visitors each year. The tourists enjoy riding the *Arrowhead Queen* paddle wheeler around the private lake, visiting the local museum and eating and shopping in Lake Arrowhead Village while listening to concerts on the Center Stage.

The movie industry continues to film movies and commercials in the area, and many in the movie industry live in Lake Arrowhead because of its proximity to Hollywood, which is less than ninety minutes away by car.

In 1995, *The American President,* starring Michael Douglas, used the old North Shore Tavern as Camp David. Nicholas's Cage's 2007 movie *Next* used the Rim of the World Highway, and the 1998 version of *The Parent Trap* with Lindsay Lohan used nearby Lake Gregory and Camp Seeley. Numerous TV show episodes and commercials are still shot in Lake Arrowhead, for the same reasons the film industry first used Lake Arrowhead during the silent film days.

Area students attend classes in Rim of the World Unified School District schools, and the chamber of commerce is very active in promoting the community. The numerous civic organizations such as Rotary, Soroptimist,

The 2014 Lake Arrowhead Village "casino" building. *Author's collection.*

the Women's Club and Rim of the World Historical Society and Museum support the Blue Jay Jazz Festival, the Arrowhead Arts Association concerts and the nearby Heaps Peak Arboretum. Lake Arrowhead remains a beautiful tourist mecca and a lovely place to live far away from the hectic world, only minutes away at the base of the mountain.

About the Author

R hea-Frances Tetley's family developed the Valley of Enchantment section of Crestline beginning in 1924, and she has been visiting the area since birth. Rhea-Frances has lived there with her family, full time, since 1976. She is a past president and a founder of the Crest Forest/Rim of the World Historical Society and is a docent at the Mountain History Museum in Lake Arrowhead. As a locally recognized historian, she has authored the column "Those Were the Days" for *The Alpenhorn News* for ten years.